Mary Ann Benson

The Natural Way to Draw
Mastery of Oil Painting
Painting Made Easy

COMPLETE GUIDE TO OIL PAINTING

THE ROAD TO EPHRATA *I painted this scene outdoors in the*
Pennsylvania Dutch country. Notice the many variations of green
and the crisp palette knife textures in the painting. (Pennsylvania
Collection, Gimbels, Philadelphia, courtesy National
Geographic Society)

Ernest Fiene

COMPLETE
GUIDE TO
OIL PAINTING

WATSON-GUPTILL PUBLICATIONS

New York

To dear Alicia with fond memories

Second Printing 1967
© MCMLXIV BY WATSON-GUPTILL PUBLICATIONS, INC., NEW YORK, NEW YORK
Edited by Susan E. Meyer.
Designed by Betty Binns.
ALL RIGHTS RESERVED.
Printed in the U.S.A.

Library of Congress Catalog Card Number: 64-14764.

PREFACE

I HAVE KNOWN ERNEST FIENE for the past twenty-five years. He has been a teacher at The Art Students League of New York for twenty years. He is a great teacher and a distinguished artist.

A great teacher must have a thorough knowledge of the principles and the techniques of his mediums. He must also be a knowledgeable humanist who can impart his own philosophy as it descends to him from the great art of the past.

Ernest Fiene's approach to the art student is fundamental, traditional, and individual. It is fundamenal in that he introduces the student to the basic materials and encourages the student to know his tools and materials, of which Fiene himself is a master.

His approach is traditional in that he believes the student should work from nature, developing his skill and sensibility.

He encourages individuality in the art student because, as a teacher for twenty years, he has seen many of his students, on the basis of the training they had with him, evolve into artists with personal points of view.

Although Ernest Fiene is a master technician, this of itself does not make a great teacher. He is a great teacher because he is a distinguished creative artist, and it is only possible for a creative artist to inspire the art student to find his own creativity.

Ernest Fiene's own life should be an inspiration to those who intend to make art their profession. He came to this country from Europe at the age

5

of eighteen, and at the time of his arrival, he knew he wanted to be an artist. He attended the National Academy of Design, where he applied himself conscientiously. From those days to now, he has consistently made contacts with distinguished artists in the United States and Europe.

His own work, in oil painting, watercolor, murals, etching, and lithography, has continuously changed, evolved, and become more masterful.

I have a great personal admiration for Ernest Fiene as a man of integrity and a great artist.

Stewart Klonis
Executive Director
THE ART STUDENTS LEAGUE
OF NEW YORK

ACKNOWLEDGMENTS

Many thanks and appreciation to Beaulah Clarkson, whose encouragement and whose revision of the manuscript have greatly facilitated the completion of this book.

Also thanks to Robert Lavine, who urged me to write this book and who was very helpful in its organization.

My appreciation to Stewart Klonis for his friendly consideration and kind words.

My gratitude to Winsor & Newton for permitting me to reproduce photographs of their equipment in Chapter One.

I also want to thank Famous Artists Magazine, published by the Famous Artists Schools, Westport, Connecticut, for allowing me to reprint so much of their material for Chapters Eight and Eleven of this book.

Paintings not credited to specific collections may be seen at the Midtown Gallery in New York City.

CONTENTS

INTRODUCTION

OIL PAINTING IS THE MOST REWARDING MEANS of self-expression in art. Oil paint is easy to handle, very flexible, and offers innumerable variations. When properly applied, oil paint is permanent.

As in all forms of creative expression, whether it is music, writing, or dance, the student must learn the fundamentals of the medium. Trial and error alone, the most difficult way to learn, is a long, drawn-out process, an approach which can lead to failure and to complete discouragement. Having studied and practiced many years, the professional artist can help you avoid mistakes and failures, so discouraging to the beginner.

This book will provide the student with the fundamental principles of the medium and will demonstrate how to use materials properly. The book will also teach you how to begin painting and how to use the basic concepts of space, composition, and color to interpret still life, landscape, and the human form.

I have not written the lessons in this book to stress one style of art over another, whether the style is realistic, abstract, or academic. The lessons concern themselves with acquiring a fundamental knowledge of the medium and the basic tenets of art expression. Painting, as a visual art, demands that the beginner interpret what he sees. With practice, study, and experience, the student will attain greater freedom and satisfaction.

This is a journey of many roads: may it be fruitful and happy!

Ernest Fiene

THE STUDIO ALCOVE
*This self portrait in
my studio shows my
palette, brushes, and
paint medium cup.
The drawings and
painting within the
painting complete
the composition
and produce an
interesting spatial
relationship.*

Chapter 1 PAINTING MATERIALS
AND TOOLS

A PAINTER works most efficiently in a large room or a studio with proper light. Although you may not be fortunate enough to have such an ideal working arrangement, you should have at least one corner where you can leave equipment undisturbed from one session to the next.

PROPER LIGHTING

Ideally, the artist's studio should have a skylight facing north which throws an even light over the room. Conventional windows are normally insufficient, because the light does not penetrate far enough into the room. Working at night, you will need some artificial illumination. A steady light coming from one direction is most desirable, particularly for painting still life, because lights coming from different directions confuse the forms, either casting too many shadows or flattening the volumes. Ordinary bulbs project a light that is too warm and uneven. For this reason, it is wisest to select a fluorescent fixture with a shell reflector, the size of which depends on your space.

Be sure to place the fixture high so that the light will fall diagonally into the room and preferably onto both your canvas and your subject. A fluorescent fixture in the ceiling which throws the light straight down distorts the form, casting shadows under all the projecting forms. So-called "daylight"

bulbs distort the color, because the light is too blue. I prefer the bulb called, "white." In a fixture of two bulbs, I use one "white" and one "daylight" bulb. Proper light is important and you should experiment with various lighting arrangements to determine which is most suitable to your work space.

PAINT BOX

Plan to get a good, sturdy paint box (12″ x 16″ is the best size) with a palette that fits inside. Art stores may try to sell you a paint box fully equipped with colors, brushes, palette knife, oil, oil cups, and painting panels, but often the selection of materials in the box is not the best. In subsequent pages, I will discuss these materials in detail, giving you my own recommendations.

The cover of your paint box will have grooves designed to hold a canvas or gesso panel the same size as the box. These grooves prevent the panels from touching one another, a feature which is especially useful when you are carrying wet paintings.

EASEL

You should have an easel. When you first start painting, you will not need the large studio type, such as professional artists use, but be sure to get a good tripod sketching easel. This easel should be sturdy enough to resist the wind when you paint outdoors. When painting outdoors, weigh down the easel with a heavy rock tied to the back leg of the tripod. At the ends of the legs, these tripod easels generally have iron spikes which can be dug into the ground. Indoors, protect your floors and rugs by setting the legs in rubber cups, obtainable at any hardware store.

ACCESSORIES

For preliminary drawings, you will need pencils, charcoal, erasers, and a chamois. By spraying fixative onto your drawing, you will prevent the sketch from smudging. You can buy fixative in a bottle—which requires a fixatve blower—or if you are short of wind but long on money, you can get fixative in an aerosol spray can.

You may want a mahlstick to steady your hand. This is a long, thin, aluminum or wooden rod which you lean against the edge of the painting to brace your hand when you are painting small, accurate details. Ordinarily, you shouldn't find the need for a crutch if you hold the brush in the middle, not close to the bristles, with the arm outstretched in a free, easy motion.

You will need a table for still life arrangements and a table or taborêt (an artist's work table) to hold your palette, paint, and brushes. Since the brushes should stand with the bristles upward, a tall vase is a convenient

EASEL   *A good tripod easel is an essential piece of equipment for the beginner.*

13

container. At the art materials store, you will find containers to hold kerosene or turpentine. Also have plenty of rags on hand for cleaning brushes, knives, and hands.

A folding screen is a useful backdrop for the studio. You can hang drapes over the screen and change the position of your background when you arrange a still life or set up a model. For figure and still life painting you should have a supply of different colored drapes to use for backgrounds. Many painters collect bottles and other objects to use in their paintings. You will probably need a smock or old shirt to protect your clothes. Remember, oil paint is not easily removed.

Have several frames on hand in your studio. Frames, canvases, and painting panels come in convenient standard sizes. While your painting is in progress, slide the picture into a frame every now and then. You can judge your painting from a fresh viewpoint when you see the picture within the confines of a frame.

PALETTE

Purchase a palette of good quality hard wood: maple, cherry, or mahogany. Cheaper palettes of soft wood are too rough and absorbent. The paint becomes absorbed into the wood, leaving behind deep color stains on the surface which are confusing when you make new color mixtures. Often the standard size paint box, 12″ x 16″, contains a palette. If this palette seems too absorbent, give it several coats of white shellac, sandpapering the surface between coats. Aluminum paint boxes (frequently preferred because of their light weight) may contain aluminum palettes coated with a white enamel which is quite stain proof. Personally, I prefer the wooden palette which, when kept well, will take on a fine finish.

For outdoor sketching, I use a 12″ x 16″ palette that fits into my paint box, but my studio palette is a large sheet of white glass, 16″ x 25″ and one-quarter inch thick, fitted onto my taborêt. This arrangement gives me plenty of room for color mixing and is easy to keep clean. However, some painters prefer to *hold* the palette while working. The traditional large, oval palette is generally used for this purpose, because of its good balance. The art materials store also carries palettes made of non-absorbent paper. Bound like drawing blocks, the sheets of the palette can be peeled off and discarded after each session. In the long run, however, this type of palette can prove rather expensive. Cleaning a palette is neither difficult nor tedious, and you will find that a wooden palette, properly cared for, improves as you work with it over the years.

Although there are infinitely more permanent colors available to the artist than appear on this palette, it is wisest to restrict the selection to a few basic colors. For the beginner, choosing colors can be very confusing. What colors should he buy, and where should the paints be placed on the palette? I have seen inexperienced students using twenty to thirty colors to paint a simple, coloristic subject. These colors were spread helter-skelter over the palette, until there was hardly space for mixing. Also, many colors canceled out one another; simple intermixtures could have eliminated one or more colors. For example, there are six cadmiums: cadmium yellow pale, cadmium yellow medium, cadmium yellow deep, cadmium orange, cadmium red light, and cadmium red deep. For an occasional orange tint, a touch of cadmium red light can be added to cadmium yellow pale to eliminate cadmium yellow deep. Other hues on the palette may be similarly derived. Remember, an experienced artist can achieve great coloristic effects using only a minimum range of colors.

The palette I propose in my diagram is designed to hold a full range of permanent, intermixable colors. The colors are placed in a succession in order to emphasize the cool and warm, as well as the light and dark, in each category. When you start a picture, you may not find it necessary to lay out all these colors. You may not need cadmium medium or cobalt blue, for example. Nevertheless, the spaces for these colors should remain empty. As you go along, you may need these colors and you can easily put them in their allotted places. Using the same palette layout every time will help you find your colors easily.

Certain vivid colors, like purple, violet, Prussian blue, "thalo" blue (a more recent substitute for Prussian blue), and "thalo" green, are generally called by their manufacturer's name; e.g. Winsor blue. Since these colors are very strong, their hue and intensity cannot be obtained by mixing other colors. I advise you to select these colors according to your taste and intentions. Violets and purples in tubes have a more brilliant hue than those mixed on the palette and they are particularly useful in painting flowers, because the hues in flowers may be so brilliant that no mixed colors can match them. Add these colors to the palette when the occasion warrants it.

What white should you buy? Cremnitz, flake, and silver whites are lead colors; they cover well, are permanent, and have shown little tendency to darken. However, these lead whites are poisonous and should be used with care. The zinc whites, and particularly the titanium whites, were discovered more recently. Zinc white does not cover as well; it has a metallic quality; it turns brittle and transparent in time, but has excellent consistency for

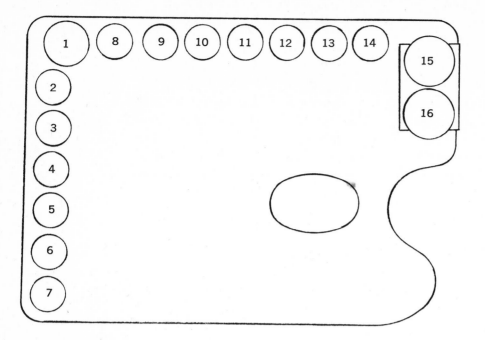

(1) White
(2) Permanent
    Green Light
(3) Viridian Green
(4) Cerulean Blue
(5) Cobalt Blue
(6) Ultramarine Blue
(7) Black
(8) Cadmium
    Yellow Pale
(9) Yellow Ochre
(10) Cadmium
     Yellow Medium
(11) Cadmium
     Orange
(12) Cadmium Red
     Light
(13) Alizarin
     Crimson
(14) Burnt Sienna
(15) Turpentine
(16) Painting
     Medium

RECOMMENDED PALETTE   *The diagram above shows the palette I
use and recommend. The colors are laid out near the edge,
allowing plenty of space for color mixing in the center. White is
placed in the upper left corner, in the most central position
between the cool and warm colors. Below the white are the cool
colors. To the right are the warm colors.*

brush painting. Titanium white is considered the most permanent white
today, but it lacks body. For this reason, it is often mixed with lead white.
I recommend the use of zinc white or titanium white for the beginner.

When setting up your palette, be sure you squeeze out enough paint.
You will need much more white than any other pigment, because it goes into
almost every mixture. When you buy your paint, select the so-called "studio"
size tubes, 1" x 4", for all colors. Because you use much more white than any
other color, the large one pound size tubes are most practical.

Generally speaking, the colors I recommend can achieve almost every
coloristic effect. Compared to the few pigments that were available to the
old masters, this is a lustrous, even extravagantly rich, palette. Nevertheless,
when you examine the works of the old masters, you will see that they did
very well with their limited means. A selection of very few colors can give

surprising results. Every color added to the palette multiplies the complexity, and control becomes more difficult. The old masters knew how to show off their limited color range by playing one color against the other, and this is a lesson you must learn, regardless of how many colors you have available.

PERMANENT COLORS

Do not place any pigments on your palette that are not permanent. Many of these "fugitive" colors are very beautiful and the temptation to use them will be great. But learn to paint without them. Even if you are not painting for posterity, you may want your picture for a few years at least.

The many names manufacturers call their paints can be misleading and confusing. When you are selecting your paints at the art materials store, pay careful attention to be sure you are purchasing *permanent colors*. For example, there is a color called lemon yellow. Since lemons cannot be ground in oil to produce a color, what is in the tube? If it is a very pale *cadmium* yellow, it is permanent, but if it is made with a cheaper pigment, such as *chrome* yellow, it is not permanent and, therefore, will darken in time. In general, you should avoid golden ochre, permanent green, and other mixed shades having similar names, unless the names of permanent pigments are specified on the tube. The more reputable manufacturers will indicate on the tube if the color is permanent. Even here, you must be cautious in your selection. An isolated color may be permanent but may deteriorate when mixed with *another* permanent color, because of chemical interaction. You must be sure that all the colors on your palette can be freely intermixed. The permanent colors for oil painting are:

White: Flake white, Cremnitz white, zinc white, titanium oxide, titanium pigment.

Black: Ivory black, mars black, lamp black.

Red: Cadmium light, cadmium deep, cadmium medium, alizarin red, light red, Indian red, mars red.

Blue: Ultramarine blue, cobalt blue, cerulean blue, manganese blue, phthalo-cyanine blue (also called "thalo" blue).

Green: Viridian, chrome oxide, phthalocyanine green, green earth, cobalt green, ultramarine green.

Yellow: All the cadmium yellows, Naples yellow, mars yellow, yellow ochre, raw sienna, cobalt yellow, strontium yellow.

Violet: Cobalt violet, manganese violet, mars violet.

Brown: Raw umber, burnt umber, burnt sienna, burnt green earth, alizarin brown.

Among the impermanent colors are the following: alizarin blue, alizarin green, all the chrome colors, and all the aniline colors. The chrome colors and vermilion should be replaced by the permanent cadmiums. The chrome colors are not to be confused with chrome oxide green, which is a permanent color. Gamboge is impermanent, superseded by cobalt yellow. Emerald green, an extremely brilliant green, is not permanent and very poisonous. (It is sold as an insecticide under the name of Paris green.) This green should not be confused with *vert emeraude*, which is the French name for viridian. Also impermanent is Indian yellow. Prussian blue, although long in use, is not entirely permanent. It is replaced by a new and permanent pigment called phthalocyanine blue. This is generally called by the manufacturer's name, like Bocour blue, or Grumbacher blue, or just "thalo" blue.

MEDIUMS

Oil paint, as it comes from the tube, has a buttery consistency, generally liquid enough for immediate brush application without the addition of paint medium. Paint should never be diluted too much, since the quality of an oil painting depends so much on its opaque character. However, there are times when you will want to add a liquid medium. For example, you may want to dilute paint to a fluid wash when you sketch in your composition. For this purpose, turpentine is a better medium than oil: not only does oil dry too slowly, but it produces an undesirable fat underpainting. Turpentine is volatile, evaporating quickly, almost entirely, and leaves no residue.

When you lay in your colors, you may want a more fluid brush stroke for which you will add a medium to your paint. In this case, never use linseed oil alone: it retards drying and causes oil paintings to darken and yellow. A more effective medium is made with two parts turpentine to one part linseed oil. To facilitate drying, add one part damar varnish. With this mixture, turpentine will evaporate, leaving no residue, and the remaining linseed oil is kept to a minimum.

Unlike the turpentine used for cleaning brushes, turpentine used for painting should be of the best quality. When turpentine is fresh, it has a clear color and an agreeable odor. When it appears cloudy and smells acrid, it should be discarded. Turpentine oxidizes and evaporates when exposed to air, sunlight, or heat, and for this reason, should be kept in an airtight container, away from the light.

If you want the painting to dry very rapidly, add cobalt calcium dryer

GLASSBLOWER TRIO   *Since glassblowers are in constant movement, I made many quick sketches on the spot, and painted the picture in my studio. I used a classical triangular composition.*

19

to the medium I have described. This dryer must be used sparingly, since its action continues even after the oil has dried. It also has a tendency to darken the colors; therefore, do not use more than ten to fifteen drops of the dryer to a pint of the mixed medium. Some artists substitute stand oil for linseed oil, because stand oil dries faster. You will find painting mediums ready-mixed at your art materials store; for more fluid painting, even these can be diluted with half turpentine.

Painters who work slowly and prefer slow drying paint mix a few drops of oil of cloves in the white on their palette. Since white is used in almost all mixtures, it retards the drying process. This is hazardous, however, and is not recommended to the beginner.

VARNISHES

Varnish plays an important role in oil painting. It fulfills two functions: it protects the painting from atmospheric conditions, dampness, and gases in the air, which may disintegrate or discolor the paint film; and it enhances the color, light, and shadow of the painted surface.

After applying several coats of paint to a picture, you will notice that the surface will dry without much gloss, lacking the color intensity you had painted. In watercolor and in tempera painting, this intensity is revived by placing glass over the painting. In oil painting, varnish fulfills the same function as glass.

RETOUCHING VARNISH

After painting *prima pura* (with one coat directly applied to the canvas), the surface of the picture will be glossy. However, when you repaint, the colors tend to sink in. As you continue to work on the painting, you will be matching the original color in succeeding layers of paint. You may find that after the picture is varnished, your new tonalities do not match the first colors at all. To prevent this, apply retouching varnish before you repaint the picture. Retouching varnish is very thin; does not form a solid or brittle coat; and can be sprayed on while you are painting. After the picture is finished and the *surface* is dry, apply a thin coat of retouching varnish. This acts as a temporary varnish until the painting is completely dry.

FINAL VARNISH

Newly painted pictures, while drying, should be kept in a dry, dust free room. Dampness retards drying and is apt to affect the surface of the paint. It is also good to keep these pictures facing the light. This helps the oxidation of oil, preventing the painting from darkening.

A final varnish (much heavier than the retouching varnish) should not be applied until the painting is six months to a year old, because the heavy varnish dries quickly and leaves a solid sheet (like glass) over the paint body. If the painting is still in the process of drying and shrinking, this solid sheet will curtail the natural oxidation of the oil by isolating it from the air and may also produce cracks in the painting.

A final varnish should fulfill certain requirements: it should be colorless; it should retain a sheen on the picture surface and protect the surface from atmospheric influences; it should be soluble; and when the picture is old and needs cleaning, one should be able to remove the varnish without damage to the painting.

There are a number of varnishes on the market made from natural and synthetic (plastic) resins. The standard varnishes for oil painting are the damar and copal varnishes. Copal varnishes leave a very hard, glossy coat which was much favored during the nineteenth century, but because copal has a tendency to darken, damar varnish is preferred today.

With the evolution of synthetic art materials, a new acrylic varnish has been developed. This is a resin made from plastic. The acrylic varnishes have been laboratory tested to be sure they fulfill the requirements listed above. The varnish is clear, like water, retaining its sheen better than other varnishes. The acrylic varnishes are not supposed to change color or darken in any way.

For artists who prefer a matte (non-glossy) finish on their paintings, there is a matte varnish to which wax has been added. This can be polished with a soft rag if a slight gloss is desired.

APPLYING VARNISH

A flat, thin, bristle brush, two to three inches wide, is the best brush for varnishing. Put the painting in a horizontal position. Place the varnish in a saucer and apply a flowing coat across the narrow width of the picture. When the entire surface is wet, stroke your brush in the opposite direction without adding varnish. To attain an even distribution of the varnish, repeat these back-and-forth strokes while the varnish is still fluid. The varnish should not be applied too thickly, but if you want a heavier varnish, repeat the same process the following day.

The best time for varnishing is during a clear, dry day at normal room temperature. The room should not be too cold or humid, and should be dust free. Keep the painting horizontal until the varnish is very tacky, otherwise the varnish may run, producing streaks on the surface.

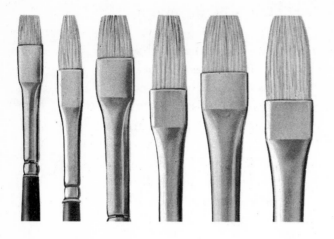

FLAT BRISTLE BRUSHES *These are the most versatile kinds of brushes.*

Sometimes paintings that have been varnished show an objectionable sheen. A coat of wax (obtainable at any art materials store) will produce a matte surface, which can be polished to any sheen desired.

Keep turpentine and varnish bottles tightly closed. Evaporation will thicken them and, in time, spoil them altogether.

BRUSHES

There are two categories of artists' brushes: bristle brushes, made of hogs' hair; and sable brushes, made from sable pelts. Your selection from the two categories will depend on the effects you want to achieve in your painting.

Bristle brushes are hard and sturdy and more generally used for oil painting. Because the bristles are stiff, they can lift a lot of pigment when you want to apply a solid coat of paint to your canvas. Sable brushes are employed for smoother textures, for detail, and for glazing (applying a thin coat of transparent color). To manipulate the paint with sable brushes, the paint must be thinned with turpentine or a painting medium. Camel's hair brushes, a poor substitute for sable, are not recommended, because they are too soft. They do not lift the paint well and they wear out quickly.

I recommend that you have a set of ten to twenty brushes. Intermix the various kinds of brushes. Experiment with them and, in time, you will know what type of brush will suit your purpose best. Buy the best quality, because a good brush is more efficient in mixing and applying paint. Good brushes are more expensive, but they will outlast cheap brushes many times: they have more spring in them, release the paint better, and you will notice that painting with them is much easier.

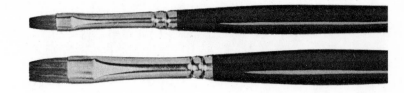

FLAT SABLE BRUSHES *These brushes are handy when you want a smooth paint surface.*

BRISTLE BRUSHES

Bristle brushes are made in three shapes: the long flat, the short square (called *bright*), and the round bristle brush. Each has its own specific use.

(The long flat is particularly adaptable to figure and portrait painting, where subtle transitions and blendings are desired. Of the three, this is the most useful, all-purpose bristle brush.)

(The short square (bright) bristle brush has its own special use. Because of its short, stiff character, the bright lifts the paint well for making heavy textures in short, thick strokes. When pressed against the canvas or panel, the brush leaves ridges of paint with each stroke. These ridges increase after several coats are applied, leaving a richly textured surface. The edge of this brush is also useful for making narrow lines and sharp edges.)

(The round bristle brush has various uses. The larger sizes cover surfaces fast because they hold a full body of paint; the small ones, carrying only a small amount of paint, are used for linear effects.)

SABLE BRUSHES

Sable brushes, round and flat, come in small and large sizes. They are used by painters who do not want heavy impasto (thick layers of paint) or uneven surfaces. (Sable brushes are also useful for glazing over rough surfaces. The smaller, round sable brushes are used mainly for linear effects and for accents (an emphatic light or dark stroke). Students using only bristle brushes should also have a small round sable, number 7 or 8, for accents and for detail. The larger the number, the larger the brush.

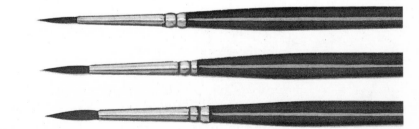

ROUND SABLE BRUSHES *These brushes are excellent for accents and linear effects.*

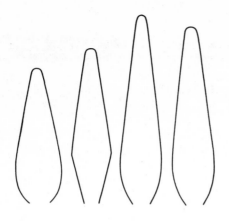

Palette and painting knives come in a variety of shapes and sizes. The diagram illustrates several blade shapes.

PALETTE KNIVES

Palette knives are made in various shapes and sizes and fall into two categories: straight knives and painting knives. The straight, sturdy knives are used for scraping paint and for mixing colors on the palette, but generally not for painting. These straight palette knives have blades about three and a half inches long.

The painting knives are shaped like trowels and are much thinner and more flexible, coming in many widths and lengths. For most purposes, a blade two and a half inches long, and not too wide, is the most useful knife. After some experience in palette knife painting, you will know how to select the knives best suited to you.

Painting knives are very delicate and their edges should remain in good shape, or they lose their efficiency. For this reason, they should not be used for scraping off dry paint on the palette or on the painting. Use only your straight palette knife for this.

Painting with the knife is an interesting and varied technique which I will discuss in greater detail in a later chapter.

CANVASES AND PANELS

The foundation (or ground) for oil painting is of primary importance. You may use the best paints and achieve a fine painting, but if your canvas or panel is not of lasting material, properly prepared, the paint will deteriorate, crack, peel, or even fall off.

For general painting and study purposes, the medium sized boards, canvases, and panels are most practical. The standard medium sizes (available at all art materials stores) are 12″ x 16″, 16″ x 20″, and 20″ x 24″. I advise you to work on these standard sizes, because you can buy ready-made frames for them. These frames are much less expensive and you will not have to wait for days until the frame you ordered is ready. For most beginners, the 8″ x 10″ panel is too small to handle with freedom. In general, a 12″ x 16″ panel would be about right for most beginners. For quick outdoor studies, I generally use the 12″ x 16″ size. For still life and figure painting, which do not have to be executed rapidly, the larger sizes can be used, but unless you are quite experienced, avoid painting on a 30″ x 40″ canvas or panel. You need a great deal of experience and time to successfully complete a painting of this size.

CANVASES

Oil painting is usually done on canvas, made of cotton or linen fiber, which is either pasted onto a board or stretched on a frame. Most painters and students buy their canvas or canvas board from the art dealer, pre-coated with a layer of white paint.

Cotton canvas is very durable and is less expensive than linen, but its weave is too mechanical and it is very absorbent. Cotton canvas is generally used by students, but most artists prefer linen, because its texture takes the paint so much better and gives more positive results.

Linen canvas comes in a variety of grains and weaves, from very smooth to very rough. The very coarse canvas is generally used for large decorative wall painting, rather than for easel painting. A canvas of even weave, smooth or medium grain, is preferable for portraits. Landscapes can take a coarser surface, because the rough grain enhances the atmospheric effect. The beginner should use a medium grain canvas. On a very smooth canvas the paint is apt to slide and not cover well, producing a slick oil cloth-like surface. On the other hand, a very coarse surface absorbs too much paint and the grain is apt to overpower the surface of the picture.

Canvas boards (also called canvas panels) are sheets of cardboard to which canvas has been pasted. Canvas panels come in several sizes. They are inexpensive, excellent for painting and sketching, fit into your paint box, and are convenient for outdoor studies.

Canvas mounted on wooden stretchers is more sensitive and resilient to the brush than canvas board and, for this reason, most painters prefer the stretched canvas.

STRETCHING YOUR CANVAS

Stretching the canvas properly takes practice, so do not be discouraged by your first attempts. Nevertheless, it is a procedure well worth learning. A canvas stretcher is a set of four wooden strips which lock together at the corners, forming a rectangular frame. Place the canvas on your stretcher (a pair of stretching pliers, sold at any art materials store, will be most helpful during this procedure) and tack the canvas onto the frame according to the following procedure.

Line up the weave parallel to the sides of the stretcher and tack down the canvas in four places, one tack in the middle of each side, drawing the canvas tight each time. When the middles of the four sides are tacked, add two more tacks to each side of the stretcher frame. The two new tacks should be on each side of the first tack, two inches away. Continue adding tacks in pairs to each of the four sides of the stretcher frame, working your way from the center to the corners. The corners are then folded under and tacked down. Be sure not to tack one whole side of a stretcher before tacking down the other side. This would result in an uneven weave, too tight in one direction, too loose in another.

PANELS

Panels are made of various materials, from cardboard to Masonite to ply-wood. These panels must be properly primed (coated with white) before you can paint on them.

To students who do not like the texture of canvas board and who are not yet ready to prepare their own panels, I recommend the already prepared gesso panels which can be bought at the artist's supply store. Some of these panels are apt to be absorbent, causing the first coat of paint to sink in. If this is the case, give the surface of the panel a light coat of thinned white shellac before painting.

For centuries, wood panels have been used for small oil paintings. The materials range from poplar to oak to mahogany. Good quality plywood panels are perfectly safe for oil painting. Be sure they are free from blemishes and do not show too much grain. Panels taken from old furniture are also quite safe.

Beaver board and other wall boards used in the building trade, are generally constructed of a paper substance in layers. They grow brittle rapidly and are too fragile for durable painting. Cardboard, light and heavy, has also been used for painting, but its permanence is very questionable.

Presdwood, also called Masonite, is a safer board to use, and in some ways, is even superior to wood panels. It is smooth on one side and rough on the other. I prefer the smooth side. Generally, the rough side is too coarse and monotonous for the picture surface; therefore, prepare the surface by applying a layer of paint with a palette knife.

RAZING BROWNSTONE HOUSES   *Demolishing old buildings is a
fascinating, colorful subject for a painting. The rich brownstone
fronts, in combination with the colored interior wall patterns,
the variety of colored doors, and the scaffolding, create an
intriguing all-over color harmony and design.*

27

KITCHEN TABLE   *This is a large rambling still life of objects that are closely related. The Dutch masters have shown that such items make interesting subjects for painting.*

PREPARING YOUR CANVAS

To hold the paint properly, panels and canvases require priming with oil paint or gesso. It is economical to prepare the canvas yourself because ready-prepared canvas is costly.

When you select raw canvas, remember that cotton is very inferior to linen for several reasons: it stretches poorly; does not take sizing or priming well; and it absorbs too much paint (which results in an uninteresting picture surface). Art materials stores carry cotton canvas which is already prepared, but this is used only where extreme economy is necessary. Linen canvas, although more expensive than cotton, gives much finer results and is easier to prepare at home.

Prepare your canvas after you have stretched it on the frame as I have already described. After you have stretched raw canvas, wet the canvas with water so that it will tighten more. Oil should never touch the raw linen or the canvas will rot, becoming weak and crumbly in time. For this reason, first apply a weak glue size which should penetrate each fiber of the canvas. Often rabbit skin glue is used, because it dries hard and resists humidity. The simplest method of making the glue is to dissolve four level tablespoons of finely ground gelatine in one pint of hot, but not boiling water. Apply this liquid glue size with a housepainter's brush—two or three inches wide— or with a sponge. When the canvas is dry, lightly smooth the surface with a fine sandpaper; then apply a second coat of sizing. No sanding is necessary after the second coat.

When this coat is dry, apply the oil priming: use Dutch Boy white lead, thinned with turpentine to a semi-liquid consistency. Be sure that there are no skins in the oil. This mixture applies nicely and should be brushed with a long, straight, smoothing stroke, in line with the canvas weave, so that the brush marks will not show. The paint body should not be too heavy; any excess can be taken off with the palette knife or paint scraper. Allow several days for the canvas to dry, after which the surface should be lightly sandpapered, and a second coat applied. Within a week, your canvas will be ready for painting. Artists generally prepare a number of canvases at the same time.

Old canvases or discarded pictures can be reused. Scrape off the ridges of paint with the palette knife and then sandpaper the surface. Then apply a coat of white lead, adding some copal varnish to the lead which will secure a better grip. The white lead coat should not be too heavy. Let it merely obscure the painting underneath. To be certain the subject you paint on this surface will not crack, this priming should dry for several weeks. The priming coat should not be heavy, so that oil colors can be applied soon after priming. Some artists reverse the canvas by remounting it on a stretcher and priming

THIRD AVENUE EL STATION AT NOON   *This is a study in perspective*
and the contrast of strong light, shadow, and color. I carefully
placed every shape and detail of the figures and cars to lend a
natural mood to the painting. (Private collection)

30

the back surface. In this way, the old paint textures do not become an obstacle to the new painting.

I would not advise that you prepare your canvas with gesso, because it is too brittle. Use gesso for panels only.

PREPARING PANELS

In preparing panels for oil painting, glue size does not have to be applied. The surface of wood panels, plywood, or Presdwood should first be sanded with a rough sandpaper, a procedure which allows the paint to penetrate the surface. Thin the first priming coat of white lead with turpentine. Then apply a heavier coat of oil paint. This should be sufficient for the normal picture surface. Paint applied to one side of a panel exerts a pull which can cause warping. To counteract this pull, apply one coat of paint to the back of the panel for each coat applied to the front. Seal the panel edges at this time. You must allow a week or so for the drying of the priming oil coats.

At the art materials store, you can buy panels prepared with gesso. These panels are generally used for oil, tempera, and casein painting. For oil painting, the gesso surface is too absorbent and must first be given a thin coat of shellac or retouching varnish.

Making gesso is a complex procedure which should be left to the expert. For this reason, I would not recommend gesso to the beginner. If you wish to prime panels, buy a jar of gesso at your art materials store.

The new water soluble acrylic paints are a good substitute and perhaps more permanent than gesso. In their industrial form, they are used for brick and cement surfaces, so that they can stand up in all weather. You can buy acrylic gesso at your art materials store. Masonite or plywood panels prepared with this paint are excellent for oil painting, and the surface does not have to be fixed with shellac or a fixative.

At the art materials store you will also find so-called *sketch boards*: heavy cardboards over which a prepared cotton canvas has been pasted. These are inexpensive and good for outdoor sketching. I would not advise using boards any larger than 16″ x 20″, because they tend to buckle. These sketch boards are very absorbent and the paint should be applied with a full brush, without too much thinner. Before you paint, you can improve this surface by applying a coat of white lead mixed with copal varnish. The varnish will make the white coat dry faster and harder. Let this dry for several days. Or if you want to use the sketch boards immediately, instead of using a paint coat, apply a thin coat of white shellac, or two coats of retouching varnish, or a coat of acrylic gesso. These dry in a half hour or so and they will help prevent the paint from sinking in.

ACROBAT MAKE-UP   *Notice the strong delineation of the foreground figure. I kept the background design to a minimum, because it added spatial interest to the composition.*

CARE OF EQUIPMENT

All professional craftsmen keep their tools and equipment in clean, efficient condition. This principle also applies to the painter. Your inspiration will soon disappear if you start painting with brushes in which the paint has dried, and with a palette containing sticky paint mixtures from the day before.

Materials and tools taken care of will also last longer, and so will your money!

CLEANING THE BRUSH AND PALETTE KNIFE

While you are painting, clean your brushes and paint knives frequently—with turpentine and rags—so that they do not carry one color into the other when you pick up paint.

The brush is a sensitive tool which loses its efficiency if it is not properly cared for and cleaned after each painting session. First, the brush can be rinsed in turpentine or kerosene (turpentine for cleaning the palette and brushes can be the cheap variety from any paint store). Then wipe the brush well with a paint rag and wash it with mild soap and luke warm water, rubbing the bristles in the palm of your hand.

When a brush loses its shape, you can restore it in the following way: after washing the brush, stroke the bristles over wet soap, then shape them with your fingers and fold a piece of paper over the hair, forming the original shape with the paper. Let the brush dry and do not use it for several weeks. Then wash out the soap and you will find the shape much improved.

To test your brush for flexibility, take a new brush and press the hair from side to side. Note that the bristles leave some space in the ferrule (the metal tubing that grips the hair of the brush); this flexibility is hard to retain but by cleaning the bristles from tip to ferrule, you maintain maximum flexibility. When the bristles get too short and stiff, the brush should be discarded immediately.

Palette knives and painting knives should also be well cleaned after each painting session. If the paint has dried on them, scrape them carefully with a razor blade, or clean them with paint remover. To be efficient, these knives must retain clean, smooth edges.

CLEANING THE PALETTE

In the first part of the book, I described how to treat new palettes. Here I shall discuss how to take care of the palette. From the beginning, you should form the habit of keeping your palette clean. Do not allow your paint to dry

SELF PORTRAIT WITH EMPIRE STATE BUILDING   *I painted this
self portrait from my studio window. The slanting wall made
an interesting pattern. I am shown drawing the unfinished
Empire State Building on a lithographic stone. Notice the
action and counter-action of the composition. The colors are
clear blue, yellow, tan, red, and green.*

34

on the palette but clean the surface after each painting session. First, scrape off the paint mixtures with the palette knife. Then clean the palette thoroughly with turpentine and a paint rag, rubbing right down into the wood. After cleaning, rub in some linseed oil, until the palette is well broken in.

Tube paint, if there is much left on the palette, can remain in place until the next painting session. The skin that may form over this paint should be removed with the palette knife before you start painting again. In case of long intervals between painting sessions, this paint can be kept fresh and wet by being placed on a tin plate or dinner plate, submerged in water. Pour off the water and replace the paints on your palette when you are ready to work again.

Palettes on which the paint has dried for a long time should be cleaned with paint remover. After such cleaning, treat your palette again with linseed oil, rubbing it well into the wood grain.

Sometimes it is necessary to clean your palette while you are still in the process of painting. This happens when the paint mixtures on your palette crowd out one another, allowing no room for new mixing. It is advisable to clean part of the palette, or even the entire surface, to prevent your new mixtures from getting muddy.

PRESERVING THE PAINTS

Keep the paint tubes closed with the caps firmly screwed on. When you take the paint from the tube, squeeze the tube from the botton. As it empties, the bottom part of the tube should be rolled up tightly. Not only will this keep the paint fresh, but you will also get the maximum amount of paint out of the tube.

If the metal cap on the tube sticks, the paint has dried. When this happens, heat the cap with a match. This will warm the oil and expand and loosen the cap. For plastic caps, use plyers to open the tube, because heat will crack the cap.

CARING FOR THE EASEL

Be sure to keep your folding easel in fine working condition. There is nothing more frustrating than finding a good subject outdoors without being able to unfold your easel. An aluminum easel is less liable to stick, but you should clean it after each session so that the paint does not dry up on it.

I prefer the heavy wooden folding easel for outdoor work. It is sturdier and holds a larger picture more steadily. It should be oiled at intervals and kept free of paint so the metal canvas holder slides without sticking.

SPRING BLOSSOMS   *In this painting, I wanted to emphasize the feeling of a crisp spring day. The pink blossoms set against the dark evergreens, and the yellow-green foliage set against the pink and blue-gray sky, give contrast and freshness to the spring scene. (Courtesy American Artists Group)*

Chapter 2 COLOR: THEORY
AND PRACTICE

SCIENCE has done much research on color theory, but it has mainly concerned itself with light rays, which are transparent. The painter is concerned with pigment, which is solid. There is an interrelationship between pigment and light rays: colored objects, like the painted surface of a canvas, absorb and reflect certain light rays. Our eyes perceive these light waves and translate them into sensations of sight.

The light of the sun and artificial light *seem* to be white, but are actually composed of light rays of all colors. These colored rays, mixed together, form white light. When light falls on an object, some of the colored rays are absorbed and vanish like water into a sponge. Other colored rays are reflected and bounce back to the eye. Thus, a red apple absorbs all rays that are *not* red. Only the red rays are reflected by the apple and seen by the eye.

The paints on your palette reflect specific colors and absorb others. Paint pigments are seldom used in pure form, but are intermixed to create the various hues, values, and intensities desired in your picture.

HUE

This word denotes color sensation: red, yellow, blue, green, purple, and violet are the sensations of color on the eye. This sensation has no relationship to the lightness or darkness of the color.

37

VALUE

The lightness or darkness of the color is called *value*. Alizarin crimson is darker in value than cadmium red, even though they are related hues. The word *value* is only used in defining the relative lightness and darkness of a color. When we mix colors, we lower the value by adding a darker color, and heighten the value by adding a lighter color. Looking at his subject, the artist decides which area is the lightest in value and which is the darkest. He then decides how to relate these areas, whether to exaggerate or subdue the contrast of values. In his painting, the artist can also decide to alter the *entire* tonal effect of the subject before him.

INTENSITY

Color intensity, also called *color saturation*, refers to the strength or weakness of a color. An object painted in pure color—any brilliant color straight from the tube (red, blue, yellow, orange, green, violet)—is more intense (more saturated) than it will be when you add other colors, black, or white.

We are all familiar with the diminishing intensity in aged materials, such as dyed cloth or an old coat of paint on a wall. Although the *hue* remains the same, the *intensity* of the original color diminishes as time passes.

In nature, objects you see in the distance lose their intensity because of the atmosphere intervening between you and the objects. This is particularly true in landscapes, where objects in the distance are more gray and blue than objects in the foreground. Fog and rain subdue the color intensity, even in the foreground. The sun's rays, on the other hand, tend to intensify the color of objects in the foreground. The saturation of these objects is reduced in the middle distance and even more reduced at a greater distance.

COOL AND WARM COLORS

Yellows and reds create a sensation of warmth, because they are akin to fire; therefore, they are called *warm* colors. Blues and greens, resembling the shadings of ice, have a cool effect and are called *cool* colors.

On the palette I described in Chapter One, I presented the broad categories of cool and warm colors. Color tints have very great but subtle effects on the eye and on one another. Even within the warm range, there are comparatively cooler and warmer tints. Cadmium red is a warmer red than alizarin crimson, because cadmium red contains more yellow. Alizarin crimson contains more blue. To test this, add white to these colors for comparison. The addition of white tends to bring out the underlying cool or warm tones.

ALONG THE EAST RIVER   *In this scene, I combined various aspects of East Side New York life, a life which is rapidly disappearing: the peddler in the foreground; the pigeon fancier on the roof; kids sledding; the inner walls of a razed building; and across the street, gas tanks, a warehouse, and the East River. The life may not be sanitary, but it is colorful and picturesque.*

39

QUEEN ANNE'S LACE AND POMODORO   *I used my palette knife for*
the entire painting, except for the slender leaves, which I
painted with a sable brush. The goldenrod enriches the
off-white blossoms. The copper lustre pitcher and the red
tomato add color and depth to the composition.

40

Try the same experiment with the cool colors: some are warmer than others. For example, permanent green is warmer than viridian, because permanent green contains more yellow, whereas viridian contains more blue. By the same token, cerulean blue is a warm blue compared with cobalt blue, and ultramarine is even cooler.

The cadmiums are another example. Warmth increases from cadmium yellow pale to cadmium yellow medium to cadmium orange to cadmium red light. The warmth *decreases* in cadmium red and cadmium red deep because yellow is absent from these colors. Black is considered a neutral color, although there are even variations of cool and warm blacks, depending on the source of the pigments. Ivory black, made from carbonized bones, is a warmer color than lamp black, made from soot. White, too, can be considered a neutral color, because all colors can be mixed with it. On the other hand, there are even warm and cool whites.

One of the first things you should develop is a mental concept of cool and warm colors. The most brilliant red, when mixed with various amounts of white, does not begin to function coloristically until it is *opposed* by a cool color, like blue or green. This is an extreme example. A very warm red, like cadmium red light, can be complemented by a yellow ochre, which is a much cooler color. At the other extreme, a gray painting can function coloristically when warm grays are complemented by cool grays.

Familiarize yourself with the effects of color on the eye: warm colors seem to be coming forward and cool colors seem to retreat into the distance. The optical effect is particularly useful in landscape painting, and will be discussed further in a later chapter.

COLOR MIXING

Whenever you mix colors, you generally change the hue, value, and intensity. The range of possibilities in color mixing is unlimited. A mixture can always be made to appear cooler or warmer by adding another color, or by placing it next to its complement.

The complementary colors are red and green, blue and orange, yellow and violet. They complement each other because each reflects the light rays which its complement has absorbed.

I said earlier that color does not function except by this opposition. I advise you to experiment by mixing colors on a palette or paper. Any attempt to measure exact degrees of these mixtures should be avoided, because doing this would detract from your freedom to improvise with color; furthermore, measurement is impossible because of the multiplicity of shades that can be mixed.

Theoretically, a hue is warmed by the addition of yellow or red, and cooled by the addition of blue or green. It is like cooling hot water by the addition of cold water and vice versa. The degree of warmth or coolness depends on the quantity of cool or warm color added.

OPTICAL GRAYS AND BLACKS

What the artist calls *optical grays* are grays produced by the mixing of any colors other than black or white.

These optical grays are actually mixtures of the three primary colors: blue, red, and yellow. The mixture of red and green produces optical grays because green is actually composed of blue and yellow. For this reason, orange and blue also produce optical grays: orange contains the primary colors, red and yellow. Optical grays can be warm or cool, depending on how much cool or warm color is combined in the mixture. A combination of these three primary colors will first appear dark brown or black; when white is added, they become grays.

So-called *optical blacks* are produced according to the same principle. Optical blacks can be mixed with various colors. For example, burnt sienna mixed with viridian or blue, and alizarin crimson mixed with green are two combinations which produce optical blacks. These blacks, used in outdoor painting, have the advantage of an airiness which is lacking in the black taken straight from the tube. I have intentionally not mentioned the raw or burnt umbers. Although they make interesting grays, they are earth colors, unrelated to the color spectrum, and their high oil content is apt to darken. It is preferable to simulate the hue of these colors by mixing other colors, like burnt sienna, green, and white.

Study the effect of color relationships: the effect one color has on another. This is a complex, elusive matter which involves your own personal reaction, taste, and imagination.

PRIMARY, SECONDARY, AND TERTIARY COLORS

The *primary* colors, from which all others colors are derived, are red, yellow, and blue. The mixture of red and yellow creates orange; blue and yellow produce green; blue and red make violet. Mixtures of two primary pigments are called *secondary* colors.

Since there are actually many different blues, reds, and yellows, obtainable in tube colors, the secondary colors can be of a great variety. To see how many blues there really are, take cerulean blue, cobalt blue, ultramarine blue, and Prussian blue, and rub each of them on white paper. Add a little

MAKING THERMOMETER GLASS   *Stage by stage, the glass is placed in various degrees of heat, from white hot to golden yellow to red. I incorporated every phase of the process in this composition. Strong contrasts of cool and warm, and light and dark produce a dramatic effect. (Collection, Abbott Laboratories, donated to the United States Department of Defense)*

43

white paint to half of each smudge. The white will reveal the great differences between the hues of these seemingly similar primary colors. Now try adding white to each of the yellows and reds. Make the same experiment by making greens, oranges, and violets from these different blues, yellows, and reds.

Tertiary, or broken hues, are obtained by mixing pigments of *three or more* colors. In these tertiary mixtures, which can be of an endless variety, the color intensity is much reduced by the intermixing of the three primary colors. White, added to certain of these mixtures, would produce optical grays. The cool grays contain more blue and yellow in the mixture; the warm grays have more red and yellow.

KEEP YOUR PALETTE SIMPLE

You can now see how varied colors can be. For this reason, keep your palette simple, or *restricted*. Study the subject you are painting as a guide for selecting the colors on your palette. This is very much a matter of personal taste, and in time you may use colors other than those on *my* palette. As long as you select only permanent pigments, you can use student colors in the beginning; they are economical for experimentation.

To gain an understanding of the elusive problem of color, start with a simple range of colors. Try executing your still life or landscape in two colors and white. Choose a warm color and a cool color, such as yellow ochre and cerulean blue, or ultramarine blue and burnt sienna. You will be surprised how many nuances of hue, value, and intensity you can achieve with only a few colors.

Then, after you have mastered this scale, add another color to your palette, such as cadmium red; later add cadmium yellow pale. Increase the colors on your palette gradually, remembering that each new color adds to the complexity and may lead to disharmony. Your taste and your sensitivity should be your guide. Use white sparingly if you want a full color effect, because white has a way of neutralizing the hue.

APPLYING COLOR

The texture and thickness of paint on your canvas are also important. A painting by a beginner is apt to look thin and colorless, probably because the student used too much paint medium and too much white. Since tube color is quite fluid, thinners (turpentine and paint medium) should be used sparingly. A dark, muddy-looking picture with a heavy paint surface is equally bad: the painter has intermixed too many colors in an attempt to copy his

44

subject. Always retain the feel of color hue in your mixtures and use the principles of opposing cool and warm shades, as I have described in an earlier section of the book.

Remember that your picture is a two-dimensional object made of pigments: a layer of paint. These pigments absorb and reflect light. In nature, light rays envelop and illuminate all objects; in your picture you are creating an equivalent with color pigments. You are reducing this large world to a canvas of limited size, with paints and not with light rays. To create an equivalent, your color must have vitality. When color dries and ages, it tends to lose vitality. For this reason, *exaggerate* the colors you see in nature, so that your painting will approach the vitality of nature when the canvas hangs on a wall under uncertain light.

LOBSTER SHACK, MONHEGAN ISLAND   *This is a rustic subject of unpainted wood. I emphasized the textures by applying the paint heavily with the palette knife. By dividing the light and dark planes in the sky, I removed the static quality this picture might have created. The rocks and boat in the foreground, and the ornamentation of lobster and net floats add grace to the total effect.*

Chapter 3 PAINTING
TECHNIQUES

46

YOU will discover that there are many ways to apply paint to canvas. The various types of brushes and palette knives produce an extraordinary range of strokes and textures. You will also learn to take full advantage of the opacity and transparency of oil paint for such techniques as underpainting, glazing, and scumbling.

BRUSH PAINTING

When properly used, the brush is a sensitive instrument of great flexibility, capable of creating a wide variety of effects and textures. For example, you can brush on the paint with a heavy impasto, or you can apply the paint thinly by rubbing it into the grain of the canvas or panel as the paint comes from the tube. Much of your success as a painter will depend on your mastery of this tool. In many ways, as with your handwriting, your use of the brush reveals your personality. A bold and imaginative use of the brush is essential to self-expression.

For me, the opaque quality of oil painting is one of its most attractive features. Except for direct sketching, or *prima pura* (one coat directly applied to the canvas) painting, an oil painting should be built up with at least two or three coats. The layers of paint lend depth and richness to the surface and the brushmarks themselves enhance the texture.

Load the brush well with paint and use the larger brushes when you lay in your subject. Vary the direction of the brush stroke in relation to the form; there is nothing so monotonous as a sky or drapery rendered with all brush strokes running in the same direction. The short bristle brush produces ridges and rich textures, whereas the long bristle brush is more suitable for smooth surfaces and the modeling of form and transitions. The round sable brush is an auxiliary to both bristle brush and palette knife. With the round sable brush you establish sharp lines and detail when necessary.

When you paint with the sable brush, you may be tempted to use too much paint medium, but remember that oil painting is not a transparent medium, like watercolor painting. Although a smooth surface is desirable, the paint body *must* remain opaque in oil painting. Sufficient oil has already been ground into the tube color to keep the paint quite fluid. Since the darkening of oil paintings is generally due to an excessive use of oil, keep the medium to a minimum. A glaze, though transparent, is a different matter altogether; a subject I will discuss in a following section.

MASTERS OF BRUSHWORK

Experience and observation will train you in the handling of the brush and in knowing which brush to employ. At the museum, take a close look at the brushwork of the masters to attain a deeper understanding of technique.

Observe how Rembrandt built up his form by his manipulation of the brush; note the various directions his strokes take, the impasto of the lights, and the modeling of the ornaments in relief. Franz Hals is probably the foremost master of the direct brush stroke. Every form is not only modeled with color and value, but with the direction of the brush stroke. These paintings were created rapidly, often in one sitting. Van Gogh is a good modern example of the same technique: the curving, writhing movement of the brush was used to create a vivid emotional effect.

Examine pictures by Monet, Pisarro, and Seurat. See how they applied the paint in short strokes. They used a short bright bristle brush, well loaded with color, and laid the paint on in dabs, leaving a very rough surface on the canvas. The light playing on this surface adds glitter to the picture. This method of painting with short strokes is particularly effective for painting foliage, and ripples on water. Seurat was called a *pointillist* because he carried points, or spots of paint, throughout his entire picture. He even went further by mixing the colors on the picture, rather than on the palette; for example, he made green by juxtaposing blue and yellow dots of paint on the canvas. The onlooker's eye mixes these colors at a distance.

The great colorists did not stir their mixtures too thoroughly, as a house painter does. In a brush stroke of violet, you can often see the component red and blue streaks. If colors are over-mixed they become dull and muddy.

HANDLING THE BRUSH

When mixing a color on the palette, many students make the mistake of spreading the color too thin and too far, as though they were actually painting on their palette. Consequently, the brush is unable to lift a sufficient body of paint, a handicap which results in a weak picture surface. Diluting such mixtures with the paint medium does not help; it results in a wash or stain rather than a solid layer of paint.

Dip the tip of your brush into the main body of oil paint on your palette, and deposit a good load of paint on the canvas. There you can spread out the paint if you want, but paint boldly! Remember, you can easily scrape off a mistake or a bad passage with your palette knife and start all over again.

In Chapter One, I recommended that you purchase an assortment of brushes. One or two brushes are not enough. Even if you clean these brushes endlessly, your colors will become muddy. Moreover, do not use a poor quality brush or a brush so worn down that it holds no paint. Often, in my class, a student hands me an impossibly bad brush to make a correction. I always say to the student, "Even Rembrandt could not have painted with this brush; how do *you* expect to paint with it?" A cabinet maker has many planes, small and large, each kept in excellent condition and each used for a different purpose. He could not possibly shape a fine cabinet without a variety of planes, any more than a painter can shape a picture without an assortment of brushes.

How many brushes should you use when you paint? In general, I think you will need about ten, in various sizes, depending on the subject you are painting. Use a different brush for each category of pigments: light and dark, cool and warm colors. For example, if you are painting a sky, you can use the same brush for all the variations of blue. You can even use the same brush for greens. But you will need another brush for the white clouds, because the light color will reveal even the slightest amount of paint residue left in your brush after cleaning.

PAINT RAGS

A good absorbent paint rag, used properly, is essential to clean brush painting. Students find this difficult to understand. They often use paper towels, or even newspapers, which are not sufficiently absorbent for cleaning the brush. Other students use an enormous rag a yard square, or an old shirt,

SAINT MICHAEL'S IN BROOKLYN   *This is an early Dutch Gothic
red brick church which I found challenging to paint. I laid
the painting in with the palette knife. When it was thoroughly
dry, I enriched the color with transparent glazes. With a
pointed sable brush, I painted the details last.*

50

day after day, until the rag becomes messy, and heavily paint-loaded. This over-exploited rag soon deposits paint on their hands and clothes and, instead of cleaning the brush, makes it muddier than ever. I advise students to tear these large rags into sections, about a foot square, and discard each one before it becomes thoroughly saturated with paint and turpentine. Since the paint rag should be very absorbent, silk stockings or nylon shirts will not do. Old bedsheets, cotton shirts, and towels make the best rags, and they are easily accessible.

You will be surprised by your improvement when you work with a good absorbent paint rag: the color will be cleaner and the painting process will be more enjoyable.

PALETTE KNIFE PAINTING

The painting knife is often used as an auxiliary to the brush. Palette knife painting is very effective, because it produces a richly pigmented surface, either smooth or rough, depending on how much paint is applied and what type of knife is employed. But using this tool properly requires practice.

Many artists paint their pictures *entirely* with the palette knife, a practice that requires precision. The palette knife painter should be a good draftsman, not working for detail but projecting the *general* pattern, design, and color quality of the subject. To a certain extent, the charm of knife painting lies in its accidental appearance; this is a deceptive quality, because painting with the palette knife demands decisiveness.

After you have some experience with color mixing and brush painting, experiment with palette knife painting. At first, repaint a discarded picture with the knife, or practice on cardboard or marginal pieces of canvas. You will be surprised when you see how much clearer the color and textures appear in contrast to pictures you have painted with a brush. Colors mixed with the brush often appear muddy and grayed, whereas those mixed with the knife show a true clarity of hue.

HANDLING THE KNIFE

A common misconception is that all palette knife painting produces a rough or coarse surface. With experience, you will find that you can paint surfaces smoother with a palette knife than you can with a sable brush. Passages painted with a palette knife have an enamel-like body and, because of their rich pigmentation, will look brilliant and stand the test of time. Vary the surface textures. Airy surfaces (such as sky and water) should be smoother than coarser ones (such as foliage and grass).

It is also effective to combine palette knife painting with brush painting on the same canvas. In a landscape painting, for example, the knife is very useful for building up strong foreground textures which, in contrast to the brush painted planes in the distance, produces an overall effect of airiness. However, the palette knife should be used with discretion in a picture where most of the painting is done with a brush, because the textures created by the palette knife take on a shinier or coarser surface, which can be very disturbing to the viewer.

With palette knife painting, you should use thick, undiluted paint. Any excess of oil in the tube can be drained off by squeezing the color onto blotting paper or newspaper. Before you start to paint, put much more paint on your palette than you would for brush painting. You will find that you use much more paint with the knife.

You can achieve very interesting effects with palette knife painting by scraping the picture while the paint is still wet. In order not to blur the picture, scrape with great caution; otherwise, one color will be dragged over another. Set the edge of your palette knife against the canvas and make a downward shaving stroke. In this way, you can scrape through various sections of color at one time, like sky, mountains, and foliage. After each stroke, clean your knife with a paint rag before starting the next stroke. An unclean palette knife will drag the sky color into the foliage, and the green into the red roof, destroying the painting entirely.

Palette knife painting should be *prima pura*; this means direct painting, not covered with a second coat. Sections you wish to repaint should be scraped off first, if there is a previous layer of paint. Otherwise, the paint ridges of the earlier coat underneath would confuse the surface of the second coat, diffuse the light falling on the picture surface, and destroy the unity of the subject. However, if you *prefer* to paint over a heavily pigmented surface, allow a long time for the first coat to dry, as long as several months. Although the paint on the surface will dry in a short while, the paint *underneath* remains wet for a much longer period of time. If applied too soon, a new coat of heavy paint will crack, because the underpainting shrinks as it dries. If you wish to change tonalities, or enrich the color values, practice glazing or scumbling over the recently dried surface.

GLAZING AND SCUMBLING

Glazing and scumbling are methods of enriching the surface of a painting. The glazing medium presents certain dangers to the novice. It requires experimentation and should be applied with great caution.

Glaze is a transparent fluid body of color. When washed or stippled over

MAN WITH ANTIQUE GUN   *I painted this colorful picture with the palette knife. The red hair and green shirt show up well against the multicolored books; the modeling of the head is firm and simple. I painted the penetrating look of the eyes without highlights.*

JANUARY II *On several occasions, I painted this view from my house. I used a palette knife for the entire picture except for the tree branches. I painted in gray, green, tan, and russet red. (Collection, Kurt von Koenigseck)*

a dry paint surface, the substance enriches the surface and unifies the picture. It is as though a piece of colored cellophane were laid over the painted surface. The color of the glaze enhances or modifies the color below, but should not entirely obliterate the foundation color.

The glazing medium consists of the following ingredients. This medium is mixed with a small quantity of tube color to form a transparent fluid.

Stand Oil—1 fluid ounce
Damar Varnish—1 fluid ounce
Pure Gum Turpentine—5 fluid ounces
Cobalt Drier—about 15 drops

All materials used in this process should be of prime quality. Enough oil paint should be added to this mixture to achieve the desired result. Apply the glaze with a soft sable brush.

If you want to tone down over-brilliance in your painting—or if you want to add solidity to a passage that seems washed out—you can add opaque or semi-opaque pigments to transparent glazes. The glaze should be well mixed in a saucer and free of any paint skins.

APPLYING A GLAZE

When you apply glaze over a large area, your painting should be in a horizontal position. Be sure that the glaze does not run. If the glaze you applied seems too rich or too thick, reduce it by dabbing the surface with a dauber of clean, lint-free cheese cloth folded into a smooth and unwrinkled surface.

Glazes may also be applied to *small* sections of your picture. You may wish to enhance or reduce a small section of red, green, or blue. In this case, mix the glaze on your palette, keep the picture in its *vertical* position—not the horizontal position recommended for glazing a large area—and apply the glaze in the same manner described above.

Some oil colors are more transparent than others as they come from the tube (like alizarin crimson, viridian, and ultramarine blue) and, in their pure states, they function as glazes. These colors, however, lose their brilliance when white is added or if they are applied too thickly. In order to bring out the full richness of transparent colors, first underpaint the object simply in white paint, so that it becomes a white shape. Underpainting in white produces a better effect than painting in a color, because a color would reduce the intensity of the glaze. When the white underpainting is dry, glaze the surface with a pure color glaze—an effect which is like laying a brilliant color cellophane over a sheet of white paper. The brilliant red draperies in many old masters were achieved by a similar method.

APPLYING A SCUMBLE

Scumbling is quite the opposite of glazing, creating a different aspect entirely. In glazing, a *transparent film* is laid over the surface. In scumbling, an *opaque color* is lightly dragged over the surface, partially revealing the color beneath. Scumbling is like a semi-opaque veil of color through which another color softly reveals itself. Scumbling paint should not be diluted with any turpentine or paint medium. Remove any excess oil from the tube by squeezing some paint onto blotting paper or newspaper. Scumble with a stiff bristle brush over the sections of the painting that need enrichment, and be sure not to obscure the underpainting entirely.

A rough surface in the painting lends itself particularly well to scumbling. If the painting pigment is spread on a rough surface, the surface will glitter because of the innumerable little ridges and valleys and broken paint textures.

If your painting is light, add a darker tint to the glaze or scumble. I do not mean to exclude using a lighter tint altogether, but a lighter tint is apt to become transparent in time, losing its effect.

There are many ways and many reasons for applying glazes and scumbles. Practice this technique on discarded pictures; you will learn a great deal.

UNDERPAINTING

Most of the old masters developed their paintings in successive layers of opaque and transparent paint. The earliest layer formed the basic design of the picture. Often, the basic forms were painted only in monochrome (one color) and white to show the patterns of light and shade. This basic structure is called the *underpainting*. Over the underpainting are painted various glazes, scumbles, and perhaps even more opaque passages.

Oil paint is not a good medium for the underpainting, because you must wait until it is thoroughly dry before you can proceed with the next layers of paint. If you do not wait, the paint may crack. In recent years, paint manufacturers have invented an underpainting white oil paint which is quite safe to use. Mixed with tube colors, this can be applied thickly or thinly and will dry in only a few hours.

I often underpaint with casein, a water soluble tempera that dries very quickly. In several weeks, casein even dries waterproof. My canvas is made of sturdy linen with a single prime (one layer) white lead oil coat. To make sure the casein will adhere to the canvas, I sandpaper the surface lightly with coarse sandpaper. The sandpapering allows the casein to penetrate.

I use chrome oxide green light and white casein for my underpainting, and I apply it in thin washes, primarily with large bristle brushes, plus a small round sable brush for accents. This underpainting must be thin because casein becomes very brittle as it dries. With changes from dry to wet weather, the canvas expands or tightens, and the heavier applications of casein tend to crack or scale off. I remove any excess paint with the palette knife while the casein is still wet.

Casein underpainting has several advantages: the fluidity of the medium allows rapid progress, quick adjustments, and compositional changes. Moreover, the green underpainting, showing through here and there, adds an airiness and a unifying color tone to the painting. The oil paint adheres solidly to the casein surface, and will not intermix with the casein underpainting. You can even remove sections of the wet oil paint, wash the surface with turpentine, and find the underpainting undisturbed.

If you wish to make the casein underpainting less absorbent, spray the surface with retouching varnish before you apply the oil paint. However, I apply the oil paint *directly* to the absorbent casein ground, and spray the first oil coat with retouching varnish. This brings out the true color values before I proceed with the painting.

TOWARD EVENING, PITTSBURGH *Cities have traditionally been subjects for painters. The obvious loveliness of Venice is well known through paintings. Even Pittsburgh has its own beauty when it is seen through the painter's eye. You can discover many attractions in your own environment. (Collection, Edgar Kaufmann, Jr.)*

Chapter 4 PERSPECTIVE, FORM, AND COMPOSITION

P ERSPECTIVE is a means of creating depth in a picture. All objects
in nature are three-dimensional: they have height, width, and depth.
A canvas has height and width, but lacks depth, so it is two-dimensional. In
order to create a natural appearance in a picture, the artist must supply the
depth. He does this by means of linear perspective; form perspective; color
perspective; form, value, and shading; and composition.

LINEAR PERSPECTIVE

Every student of art should have a rudimentary knowledge of perspective.
This does not imply that you must apply the scientific principles of perspective to every picture. Many contemporary artists intentionally use a distorted
or arbitrary perspective in their work; but all good artists are well aware—
or should be—of the principles of perspective.

First observe perspective in nature: you will see that shapes diminish in
size as they retreat into the distance. Notice that the railroad tracks get
closer and closer together in the distance, until they seem to touch on the
horizon. You know this is not so; it is a visual illusion. The same diminution
of size can be observed in all other objects. Both the height and the width
of objects—like a row of telephone poles—diminish as they recede in the
distance. The poles are all of the same height and thickness, but their height
and thickness seem to diminish gradually as they retreat from view.

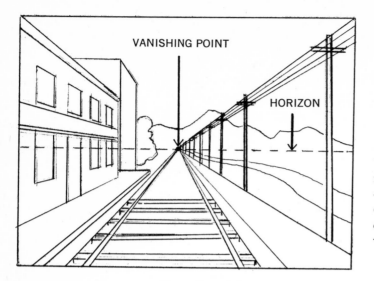

VANISHING POINT

HORIZON

PERSPECTIVE WITH ONE
VANISHING POINT *The rails
on this railroad track seem to
converge as they arrive at
the horizon line. The height and
width of the vertical telephone
poles seem to diminish in
size as they recede into the
distance. Note that the poles
and tracks converge at the same
vanishing point.*

On a flat plain or at sea, you can observe the horizon clearly. The horizon is the place where the sky and the land or water meet. When you are standing on flat land, the horizon is always at eye level. In hilly or mountainous country, the horizon is less easily observed, but you must *imagine* a horizon line at your eye level. All retreating lines from above the horizon move downward to meet the horizon line, and the lines from below the horizon move upward to meet the horizon line. The point at which these lines converge is called the *vanishing point*. There can be several vanishing points in one scene. Objects in a landscape, for example, can point toward various vanishing points, depending on the placement of these objects.

The position of the horizon line depends on the height from which you view this line. It is always at eye level, whether you view it from a high or low position. From a high building, the horizon seems higher than it does from street level. A sailor on a high mast sees a more distant horizon than a sailor on deck.

The principle of horizon line and vanishing point remains the same even indoors. In an enclosed room, the distance is not great enough for you

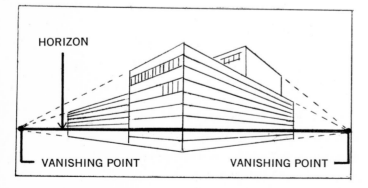

HORIZON

VANISHING POINT   VANISHING POINT

PERSPECTIVE WITH TWO
VANISHING POINTS *The number
of vanishing points in a
picture is determined by the
number and placement of objects.
In this architectural scene
there are two points at which
the lines converge.*

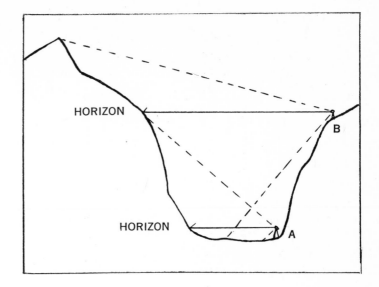

FIELD OF VISION *When you stand at the base of a mountain (A), your field of vision is very limited and the mountain seems small. When you stand at the top of a hill (B), the same mountain will look larger, because you have a wider field of vision.*

to see the converging lines meet the vanishing point on the horizon. *Vertical* lines do not change, unless you look upward into a canyon of skyscrapers. In this case, your eye creates a new vanishing point, towards which the skyscrapers seem to be converging in mid-air.

Photographs tend to exaggerate perspective, because they enlarge foreground objects and diminish distant objects. This exaggeration makes photography an excellent medium for studying perspective. Take a photograph of a street scene and, with a ruler, draw the retreating lines of the rooftops, windows, and ground lines, in order to find the horizon line. If there is enough distance in the photograph, you can also find the vanishing point. Furthermore, you should be able to tell from what height the photograph was taken, because the lens level corresponds to the eye level. Try the same experiment with photographs of room interiors and landscapes.

FORM PERSPECTIVE

So far, we have considered linear perspective, the perspective of lines in space. *Form* perspective involves diminishing *volumes*. In a still life, oranges of the same size, placed behind one another, diminish in size. Buildings appear smaller in the distance than they do in the foreground. Figures also diminish in size as they recede, regardless of whether they are indoors or outdoors.

Another kind of form perspective is called *foreshortening*. Foreshortening occurs in figure and animal forms as well as in inanimate objects. A leg or arm pointed towards you is not seen in its full length, but is foreshortened, receding into the distance.

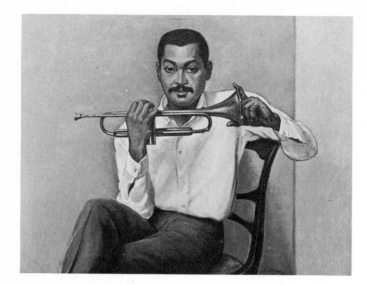

PORTRAIT OF ART FARMER *Notice how the legs and arms have been foreshortened. The left forearm, for example, looks shorter in proportion to the torso, creating the impression that the arm is coming towards you.*

COLOR PERSPECTIVE

Perspective affects not only the size and position of objects, but their color as well. In landscape, notice that colors change as they retreat into the distance. This change is due to the intervening atmosphere. In the foreground, the colors are strongest: in the distance, the hue diminishes, turning grayer and bluer. For example, mountains in the distance, although densely covered with green foliage, appear blue; black looks gray; red (the color least affected by atmosphere) looks paler and grayer.

Naturally, there are exceptions. For instance, heavy clouds tend to mute the colors in a landscape, but suppose sunlight breaks through the clouds, illuminating a section in the *middle* distance. The sun patch heightens the color in the middle, and the foreground is *less* brilliant.

Study the works of the impressionists (particularly Seurat and Cézanne) to see how they mastered color perspective. Cézanne used blue outlines, from light to dark, to render the feeling of depth and perspective in his pictures.

Colors also carry a certain psychological association which can be used to enhance the perspective of your painting. When painters speak of advancing and retreating colors, they are referring to the warm colors, which appear nearer to us, and the cool colors, which appear further away.

But cool and warm colors can cause complications. You may have followed the rules of line and form perspective, but the natural colors in your scene may counteract the sense of depth you are trying to achieve. For example, in the foreground of your scene there is a blue house and in the distance, brilliant autumn red foliage. How can you prevent the blue from retreating into the distance and the red from advancing to the foreground?

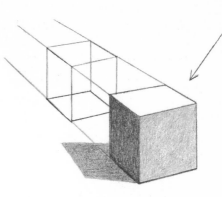

THREE BASIC VALUES ON CUBE
In a cube such as this, you can clearly see the three basic shading values: light, halftone, and dark. The edges and flat planes sharply differentiate one tone from the other. Note how the light source (indicated by the arrow) affects the density and direction of shading.

With experience, you will learn how to adjust and relate colors by subtly altering their line, value, and intensity to "keep things in their place." However, there are occasions when an object, generally man-made (like a distant bridge that has just been painted red), simply will not stay in its place in the picture plane. You then must choose between changing the color, or not painting the subject at all.

SHADING AND VALUE

Creating the illusion of depth in your painting, you must convey a sense of volume to all forms. Apples, faces, trees, *all* objects have volume. Even a cloud is a volume of vapor that occupies space, and this sheet of paper, thin as it may be, has height, width, and depth. In painting, you must learn to transpose these natural forms to your canvas.

One way to produce the sensation of volume is by *shading*. Since the patterns of shading from light to dark are created by the light falling on an object, you must study the relationship of shading to light direction.

A ball illuminated from *every* direction is formless, visually reduced to a flat circle. A single source of light, on the other hand, produces shadows on the sides of the ball which are *not* directly facing the light. These shadows give volume to the object. That is why, in still life painting particularly, a single light source is very important. In outdoor painting, the light comes from a single source, the sun, and even on a cloudy day the direction of the sun's light is visible.

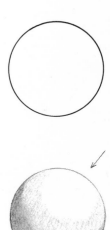

LIGHTING ON SPHERE *Illuminated from all sides, the sphere at top loses the appearance of volume. Shapes are flattened: the billiard ball looks like a disc. The ball in the middle shows three areas of tone: light, halftone, and dark which are then subtly blended into one another, producing the effect of volume, shown at bottom. The arrows indicate light sources.*

Using a cube as an illustration, you can see most clearly how light and shade are related. Only three planes of the cube are visible at any one time, and each plane has a distinct value: light, halftone, and dark shadow. Because of the sharp edges and flat planes of the cube, these three values are clearly defined.

Values in a round shape are more subtle and varied; complex and irregular shapes are even more difficult to observe and delineate because they show a greater variety of shadings. If you attempted to paint the many subtle values that appear in complex shapes, you would end in utter confusion. For this reason, the artist limits himself to the three fundamental shading values defined in the cube—light, halftone, and dark—no matter how complex the shape appears.

All other values are considered incidental. They come about at the point where shade blends into halftone, and where halftone blends into dark. They are also caused by reflections and highlights falling on an object.

To illustrate how this happens, try drawing a billiard ball. You can begin by drawing the three values—light, dark, and halftone—as three areas of flat tone. However, these three flat areas will look like stripes on the billiard ball if you do not blend them into one another. By blending the dark into the halftone, and the halftone into the light, you add two more values at the transition points, giving you five values altogether. If the billiard ball is standing on a light surface, a light reflection on the lower edge of the billiard ball is apparent. Still another value is introduced.

You understand that this is a simplified equation; it is actually impossible to measure *exactly* how many values arise when we blend the dark plane into the light. That is why it helps to limit yourself to the three fundamental values when you shade a form. In the process of blending, you should be careful to retain these three basic values; otherwise, the form will be lost. A white teapot, a tree or rock formation have complex forms; your picture would look confused and unconvincing if you did not approach shading in this simplified, schematic way.

At first, make black-and-white drawings in shading of various simple objects (in pencil or charcoal), then gradually progress to the more complicated forms. After you attain ease in shading in black-and-white, it will be less difficult for you to model in color.

SEEING FORMS AS TRANSPARENT   *Study objects as though you could see through them. In this way, you will develop an understanding of form.*

FORM

So far, we have concerned ourselves with shading objects. In order to make these objects convincing, you should know as much as possible about their *form*. When you draw a cube, you render only the three planes you can see. Pick up this cube and you will notice that there are other planes you did not see. Try visualizing the cube as glass and draw it through to the other side. In a water glass, because of its transparency, you see the front and back plane at one time. All objects are displaced in space, and you should know how they look from *all* angles, not only from the front view.

Understanding this principle requires a lot of thoughtful observation and practice. Make many diagrams, drawing the form as though it were transparent, through to the other side, top and bottom. Cut an apple in half and note the dissected form. Mentally dissect solid shapes, like buildings, boxes, a dresser, a chair, a vase, rocks, or tree trunks. The more you know of form, the better you can render it convincingly.

There is a bewildering mass of shapes in nature. In attempting to bring order into the forms in his pictures, Cézanne discovered that many objects in nature could be reduced to basic geometric forms: sphere, cube, cone, and cylinder. Observe objects around you and see if you can reduce them to their basic geometric forms.

FOUR BASIC GEOMETRIC FORMS
The sphere, cube, cone, and cylinder are four basic geometric forms out of which most objects are derived. Study the possible variations you can achieve from the fundamental shapes.

COMPOSITION AND SPATIAL RELATIONSHIP

The painter is always confronted with the problem of selecting, from the infinite space around him, the ingredients which will produce an interesting canvas. For example, in a still life, the wall directly behind the objects continues all the way to the ceiling; the table extends to the floor. There may be a chair or window on either side of the table. How much will you include in your limited canvas space? Is your subject better suited for a horizontal or a vertical composition? These are questions which require an understanding of spatial relationship and composition.

Set up your still life and distribute the various objects until you find a combination that is pleasing to your eye. Next consider how the objects will be placed on the canvas. Create the composition as you draw your subject.

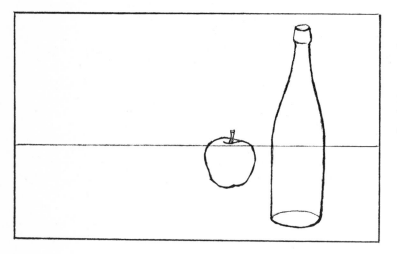

UNBALANCED COMPOSITION *This illustration is an obvious example of imbalance: arrested at the right side of the picture plane, the eye is unable to perceive the composition in its unity.*

STATIC COMPOSITION *In this illustration, the space is divided so equally that the composition appears static. The eye cannot move freely from one space to the other.*

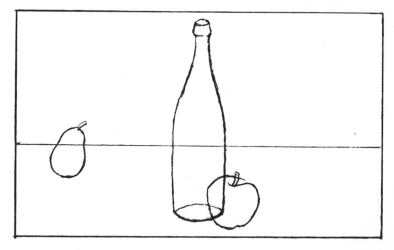

The artist thinks of the picture plane (the rectangular surface of the canvas) as a self-contained world that does not extend beyond the frame. This world consists of spaces divided into various patterns; movements controlled by thrusts and counter-thrusts of the objects in the painting.

Directional thrusts and counter-thrusts are created by the placement of objects, which divide the plane into patterns and spaces. The interplay of shapes and spaces, called the *spatial relationship*, can be balanced or unbalanced, depending on how the spaces are composed. Whether the objects in your painting are fruits and bottles, trees and mountains, or portraits and figures, they should be arranged in such a way that they enable the eye to move freely in the picture plane, without being forced away by movement or thrusts that unbalance the composition.

In this chapter, you will find diagrams that illustrate how essential good

UNBALANCED LIGHT AND DARKS
The composition is unbalanced in this picture because all the dark forms are placed on the right side of the picture, the light forms on the left. The arrows show the thrust and counter-thrust of the shapes in the composition.

BALANCED COMPOSITION *Here the picture is much improved by the use of light and dark shadows, evenly distributed, to balance the composition. The drapery is introduced to establish this balance.*

67

composition is to a successful painting. There are an infinite number of possibilities in composition, so I advise you to shuffle around the objects in each of your paintings.

The distribution of spaces or patterns (created by the objects) should be varied and harmonious to hold the eye in the picture. The eye should not be cornered into one section of the picture, unable to move from one space to another. The eye is trapped when the spaces in the picture are divided too equally; or when the picture is cut in half by a diagonal line, or vanishing point; or when there is an imbalance of light and dark. I do not mean to preclude the dominance of a single object in your painting, but the major object should be part of a balanced composition, not centered or static.

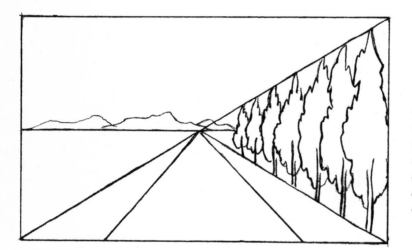

COMPOSITION CUT IN HALF *The composition in this landscape is* poor, *because the picture is cut exactly in half. The diagonal created by the edge of the road and the tree tops leads the eye out of the picture.*

COMPOSITION TRAPS EYE AT VANISHING POINT *Here again is a composition of equal divisions. The eye is trapped by the vanishing point in the center of the picture. The eye will soon tire of studying each half of the picture separately.*

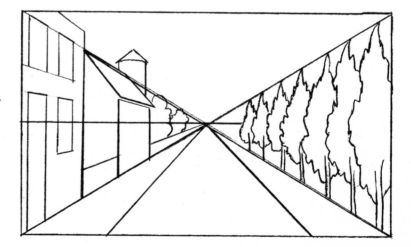

68

VARIED AND HARMONIOUS COMPOSITION *This landscape composition shows improvement. The distribution of space is varied and harmonious, encouraging the eye to move from one section to another, always within the confines of the picture. The dominant object (the group of trees) is not centered, and the surrounding space is made interesting by the diagonal patterns.*

Practice with composition by making small pencil sketches within a defined outline, representing a picture plane. This outline can be square, oblong, horizontal, or vertical: feel free to alternate the shapes. At first, draw only one object in the space, giving it maximum decorative value. Remember, that the empty spaces surrounding the object are also significant. How much of the space shall the object occupy? Where will the horizontal line of the table be placed? Gradually include more objects in your sketches, varying the combinations.

Study the work of the masters and see how many ways they composed their pictures. The variations are infinite. Experiment with space divisions until you can recognize an unbalanced composition and correct it easily.

Chapter 5 STILL LIFE

PAINTING

I N THE foregoing chapters, I have discussed some of the general technical and theoretical aspects of painting. Now is the time to put these ideas into practice by painting a picture.

I advise the beginner to start with still life painting, because still life is the first step toward the study of nature. The objects are stationary; the light is constant; and there is no time limitation. At your leisure, you will be able to experiment with your palette, with mixing and applying paint to your canvas. There is so much to learn, through trial and error, that if you started with landscape (and its changing light) or with figures (constantly moving) you would become discouraged and confused. When you begin to paint, you need time to check the accuracy of your color mixtures, and to compose your picture. After you have had some experience, and feel more secure in the handling of your medium, you can advance to more complex subjects. But begin with still life.

In still life painting you can go back, day after day, to the same subject. Doing this, you can see many nuances you missed before. Colors mixed on your palette will look different when you apply them to your canvas. Many surprises await you. A subject in nature whose color and composition may seem pleasing in nature may look scattered and inharmonious on your canvas. Only through practice and experience will you learn how to adjust to this alteration.

SELECTING YOUR SUBJECTS

When you set up your first still life, select simple subjects that do not deteriorate or transform rapidly. Paint perishables, such as flowers, vegetables, or fruit, only after you have gained some control of the medium. You can find an abundance of non-perishable objects all around: vases, china, crockery, kitchen utensils; in fact, any object you like will do. The rummage store, the Salvation Army, or an antique shop can provide unusual articles, as long as you choose your subjects with care.

Arrange still life objects according to your taste, but remember that certain things are more appropriate together than others, whereas other combinations can look incongruous. Still life subjects invariably suggest associations which can even be employed as symbols. The colors, shapes, and textures of the objects may harmonize, but if conflicting ideas are suggested, the picture can be very disturbing. You can set up a still life of objects from the sea—fishes, seashells, and a copper pot—but a Dresden china figurine would look very strange in such a composition. On the other hand, a hunting cap and gun would go well with wild fowl or game; vegetables with kitchen utensils; Dresden china with fine lace, or any other number of combinations.

Exercise the same selectivity in flower painting. Wild flowers would look more natural in a coarse vase than more delicate, cultivated flowers. Consider other accessories also: the finish and wood texture of the table top; drapes or table covers; and other objects incorporated in the composition.

Use your own taste to guide your selection and also study the works of the masters, where you may find interesting still life accessories.

You can paint the same still life several times on the same canvas or on a new one. When you get tired of this, set up a new still life, entirely different from the first one. Until you have gained some freedom in handling the paint, I would not advise you to attempt too elaborate a subject.

Some painters keep several still life set-ups in their studio for days and weeks. They return to the still lifes again and again, always finding new interpretations of the same subject.

COMPOSING YOUR STILL LIFE

It is difficult to put into words what makes a good composition or how to achieve balance. Since there is a multiplicity of possibilities, there can be no rules. Experiment by juxtaposing the objects you have selected until you find a pleasing and harmonious grouping. After you have made a small sketch of this composition, again shuffle around the objects for another possible combination. Sketch each composition. From these drawings, select the best composition for your painting. In the preceding chapter, I proposed some rules of composition. Use these rules as an aid in making your decision, but rely on your innate sense of balance. If you know your picture is out of balance, you should be able to figure out a way to correct it.

Remember that the patterns *surrounding* your objects are equally significant. Study the relationship of the objects to the background and make any appropriate changes: pin up the drapes; cover the whole background; divide the background into a pattern harmonious with the composition. You do not have to be literal; if the wall behind the table is gray, you can paint it a gray-green or pink, if this color suits your picture better, as long as your colors are in the same value. If you use a different value for your background, your objects might be silhouetted too sharply.

Study the perspective of the table top and the objects on it. The objects should fit well in your picture, neither so large that they overpower the picture, nor so small that they get lost.

BEGINNING TO PAINT

Begin your painting modestly. Paint either standing or sitting, but always stay in the same position when you paint still life, because the perspective changes everytime you view the subject from a different angle. The standing position has one advantage: you can step back frequently to see your painting and your subject from a distance to compare the accuracy of your shapes, colors, and values.

Keep your palette on the table or taborêt, within easy reach, so that you can paint without changing your position. Many painters prefer to hold the palette, but I believe your motions are freer when the palette is on a table.

In the beginning, confine yourself to the smaller size canvases or boards, 12″ x 16″ or 16″ x 20″.

The first day of painting should be devoted entirely to working out the overall composition and laying in the broad masses of the still life. Take the preliminary sketch you have selected and draw it on your canvas with charcoal, rather than pencil. Seeing your still life sketched on the canvas may cause you to shift an object on the table, or recast your composition entirely. Charcoal is the best drawing utensil to use, because you can easily make quick changes and wipe out sections. After you have completed the composition, spray the charcoal drawing with fixative. Or you can paint over the lines of the drawing with blue or ochre paint, very much thinned out with turpentine, and then wipe off the charcoal.

Using large brushes, paint the forms in light and dark color values and lay in the entire composition, including the background and table, without

STEP 1 *When you set up your still life, distribute the objects*
so that they are well balanced. If they are too scattered, the overall
arrangement will lack harmony. By overlapping the shapes, you
can tie objects together in order to give depth to the picture.
Notice how I have overlapped the white coffee cup in front of
the dark lustre pitcher. I used the same device with the two lemons,
the orange, and the brioche next to the book. The diagonal
placement of the table cloth, and its folds, further ties the objects
together. I painted in cobalt blue, thinned with turpentine. I laid
in the general color of the background, gray yellow, as the first step
to developing a color harmony.

74

STEP 2   *After I completed the design, I gave my full attention to the flowers, because they change so rapidly: the buds open and the large roses lose their freshness. After the flowers were well established against the background, I laid in some of the other colors on the objects, stressing in particular their shadow patterns. The shadows indicate the direction of light and enhance the volume of the objects.*

75

STEP 3   As the painting proceeds, the outlines are absorbed by
the modeling and coloring of the forms, giving depth and air
to the canvas. I carefully delineated the different textures of the
cloth and wood, of the fruit and lustre pitcher. To give harmony
to the picture, I closely observed and adjusted the color values
to one another.

76

STEP 4   *In the final stage, I softened the edges here and there, and accented other parts. Highlights and detail, kept to a minimum, were added. The still life is now completed. The vitality of the painting is achieved by composing the objects harmoniously, distributing the colors, and accentuating the textures.* (THE BREAKFAST TABLE, *Collection, Mr. Daniel W. Meyer*)

painting too much detail. After the canvas is covered, you can then concentrate on the finer values.

Keep the detail at a minimum. As long as you keep the colors fresh and bright, enjoy your work and do not feel you must be literal about matching them. The relative color values and hues will not be apparent until your canvas is completely covered, at which time you can make your adjustments.

THE SECOND SESSION

When you return the following day, you may find that the paint has dried in flat, preventing you from seeing the true values you painted the day before. Before continuing any further, blow on some retouching varnish, which will restore the true hue, value, and intensity. The varnish dries quickly, so you can begin to paint again in a short while.

First, make color adjustments: increase the intensity of some hues, decrease others, and change the values here and there. You may wish to sharpen edges and soften others or even to rearrange some of the objects in the composition or to change the color of the background. The real fun of painting begins now.

During the second session, you should still refrain from putting in the detail. For most students, this is a hard discipline to follow, because the detail or ornamentation of an object is so attractive that it frequently overwhelms the object itself. Often I have seen students paint the ornamentation on a vase while the vase itself was still only an outline. This is wasted effort because the ornamentation will only be destroyed when you model the form of the vase. It helps to consider all forms and their relationship from an architectural point of view: as masses in the picture plane. The architect first designs the general plan of masses and proportions before he draws in the windows, moldings, and doors. The artist conceives his painting in the same way.

Although you may not want to change the overall composition, there is still a great deal that needs development in the second session. In the excitement of painting, it is easy to make errors; they can be corrected later. Build up the solidity of forms, develop a better color harmony, and adjust the textures. Do not be afraid to experiment. You can scrape out sections (or overpaint them) and brighten or lower the color scheme.

HANDLING COLOR

As I have discussed in Chapter Two, the colors of objects change radically, depending on how they are juxtaposed to other colors: a dark green bottle

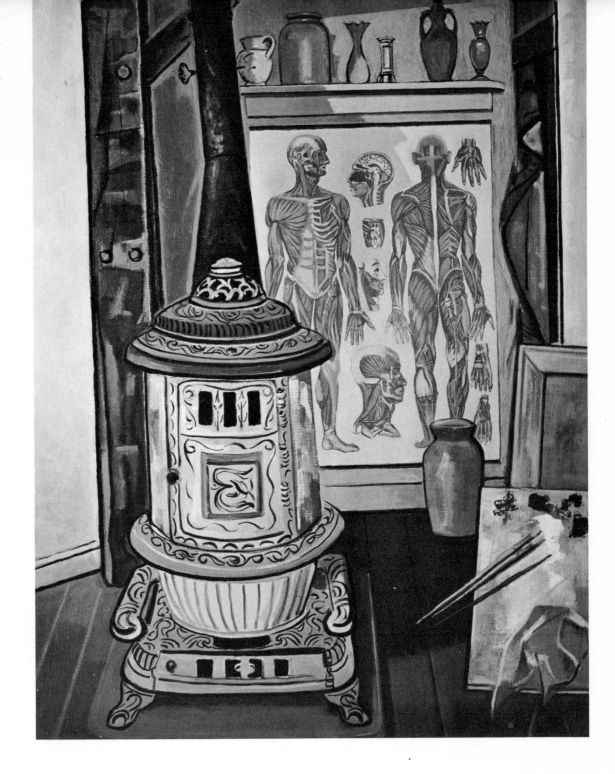

THE STUDIO ALCOVE   *This section of my country studio contains various objects I have collected as possible subjects for paintings. The old woodburning stove is a great asset on cold winter days. The anatomy chart, palette, jugs, and vases complete the studio environment.*

79

GOLDENROD IN LUSTRE PITCHER *One of my favorite painting sub-jects is wild flowers. Two complementary primary colors, the yellow goldenrod and the pale blue background, in turn comple-ment the dark copper lustre and the violet pink of the thistle.*

80

looks darker against a light background, yet greener against a pink background, or lighter against a very dark background, and even grayer against a rich green background. In fact, color does not exist *except* by these contrasts.

Generally, an object with warm color in the light plane has cooler colors in the shadow plane; an object with cool colors in the light plane has warmer colors in the shadow plane. When you start to paint, you will attempt to put the theories of Chapter Two into practice.

Do not be afraid to experiment. Paint broadly, applying the paint richly, with good size brushes. With some practice, you will learn how to see even a monochrome wall in a more subtle way. You will see that a wall may vary in tonality: an object against the wall may cause the wall to darken; against the shadow plane of the same object, the wall appears lighter. Even the *color* of the wall may change, depending on the color of the object you place in front of it.

PAINTING TEXTURE

Texture is an important part of pictorial expression and affects the rendering of edges and highlights. Objects reflect and absorb light the same way colors do. An earthenware jug with a pottery glaze will *reflect* light, whereas one without the glaze will *absorb* the light.

If you paint a still life of a red apple, a green pear, a banana, and an unglazed pottery jug, you will discover the following: the red apple, having a very smooth surface, reflects light, mirrors the colors of the objects next to it, and shows a bright highlight. The banana, having a soft texture, does not mirror the color of the adjacent objects and shows little, if any, highlight. The pear, if unpolished, will show a soft highlight, and hardly any reflections on its surface. In the same way, the unglazed pottery jug will absorb the light, without showing *any* highlights or reflections.

It is worth noting that texture does not eliminate the three values of light, halftone, and dark. Although textures may vary, all shapes show the light, halftone, and dark values that I discussed in the preceding chapter.

Picture in your mind the differences between polished silver, a silk cloth, a woolen blanket, and a thick fur. You should simulate these differences with your brush. But how? One way to evoke texture is by applying thicker and thinner layers of paint to effect a smoother or coarser surface. Because of the beginner's general timidity, I suggest you exaggerate these textural differences by making the smooth surfaces smoother and the rough rougher, *not* by painting in detail or by dotting the surfaces. Apply good solid paint, particularly in the light areas. In the darker sections of the object, use thinner paint and emphasize textures less. When the picture is placed in another light, heavily painted dark areas may catch too many glints of light, an effect which would destroy the unity of the dark plane.

Textural differences are achieved not only by the application of rougher and smoother layers of paint, but also by the direction of the brush stroke. In the textures of furs and in wood grain, you can notice a certain movement or direction. Observe the movement of the texture and follow this movement with your brush stroke. The direction of the stroke can also be applied to show the form of an object: a square object would take a straight brush stroke; a round object would take a curved brush stroke to emphasize its form. Van Gogh often used this arbitrary device to enliven his paintings and to emphasize form and movement.

Even a flat wall background should show variations of texture. Do not mix only one color, applying it to the background the way a housepainter does. Vary your strokes and colors.

PAINTING EDGES

Observe the edges of the objects in your still life. When you first lay in the painting, keep all the edges soft, undefined. As you develop the picture, sharpen some of the edges and keep others soft, depending on which object you are painting. Some objects have, by nature, hard edges; others soft, according to their textures. Metal and glass objects have hard edges; wool has a soft edge; the edges of an orange are not as soft as wool; the edge of a shiny apple may be as hard as glass. Look for these differences. Even a hard object can show a softer edge here and there, and a soft object can show a sharp edge here and there.

If you accent all objects in your picture with the same hard outline, the objects will separate themselves from one another, eliminating the depth and unity in the painting. Look at your still life set-up to see how naturally and harmoniously it rests in space and then attempt to capture this quality in your painting. It is important to handle the edges of the objects properly. Once the composition is established, your use of color, form, texture, and varied edges is more important than your emphasis on detail.

PAINTING HIGHLIGHTS AND CAST SHADOWS

Also observe the highlights in your still life painting and be sure not to over-emphasize them. To many students, the highlight on a form is shown by merely a dab of pure white. Actually, there can be a great variety of highlights, ranging from dim to bright, depending on the color, texture, and surface density of each object.

82

MALLOWS WITH T'ANG HORSE   *The large pink mallow, its dark leaves, and the deep purple Mexican glass, placed against a rich blue background, all complement this ancient Chinese horse. The exotic quality of this painting is in keeping with the subject matter. (Collection, Mrs. Carol Brandt)*

83

Not only the strength, but the *color* of the highlights may also vary, depending on the color of the light source. For example, in a studio with north light, the highlights are often blue, because they reflect the sky. Since all the objects in a still life should be bathed in the same light, it is essential to study the highlights in relation to the light source.

Also observe the cast shadows, their direction, and density. They should not overpower the form, but complement it, creating a unity in the picture plane. "Theatrical shadows," a term used by artists, is a derogatory way of saying that very heavy shadows are artificial and over-dramatized, a device used by superficial painters, who over-accent the shadows in an attempt to create the illusion of form where no form exists at all. Do not allow yourself to fall in this category.

LOOKING FOR COLOR AND FORM

Your first still life may lack form and color. Build up three-dimensional forms with strong contrasts of the planes, light, halftone, and dark. Give full brilliance to your color, even exaggerate the brilliance. Hold up a small mirror in such a way that you can see both your still life set-up and your picture at the same time. Seeing them in reverse, you quickly discover your oversights and mistakes.

When you paint objects for the first time, forget what you already know about them, because this can be a hindrance to your approach. Study the form you are painting, but be unaffected by the associations it carries. This is not to say you should take a photographic point of view! The eye and mind will see differently than the camera, in spite of so-called "objectivity." You will also see things differently from the person next to you. Thirty students in a class, painting the same subject, will paint thirty distinctly different pictures.

There is no patent or formula for painting anything. The experienced artist can help you see, and guide you in the intricacies of color mixing and painting techniques. Essentially, however, you are on your own: you must practice seeing, painting, and expressing yourself.

Painting glass and water is an excellent way to exercise your painter's eye. Although glass is considered colorless and transparent, you can paint it, because you can see it. The tonalities are so subtle that you are compelled to exercise all your visual faculties to render it.

First, notice that the glass has structure and design. For example, the surface of a water glass may be very smooth, plain, or it may be ornamented and rough. The glass itself may be very thick, compared to a thin wine glass. The water glass, having thicker edges, would seem slightly more opaque than the wine glass. The pattern and density will change completely when you fill the glass with water, even though water is also considered clear and transparent. Put a spoon in the water and notice how its shape appears distorted. Make a drawing of the glass with charcoal or soft pencil.

Try placing the glass in front of a white background, studying the patterns and shadings created on the white and on the glass itself. Standing against a white background, the glass reveals highlights which are lighter than any other tones, including the tones in the water itself. Since white is the lightest color on your palette, it follows that all the other shadings, including the white background, should be a darker tonality. The other colors you select are determined by what kind of light is falling on the glass and the color behind and under the glass. So you see, there are many variables in painting even in two so-called *transparent* and *colorless* objects such as water and glass.

STUDYING STILL LIFE MASTERPIECES

Do not regard still life painting as merely a convenient exercise. Some of the great masters used still life as a final subject in their paintings: Caravaggio, Chardin, Cézanne, Picasso, and Braque, to name only a few. Still life has enabled artists to explore changing concepts of space, to comment upon their environment, and has acted as a vehicle for emotional expression. Still life is not just an exercise: it can be a complete work of art in itself.

The greatest still life painter of modern times was Cézanne. In fact, Cézanne saw all of nature as a still life, being so deeply interested in form, and the interpretation of form with color. After ninety long sittings, Cézanne completed his portrait of Ambrose Vollard, a French art dealer. The portrait had been a trying experience for the model: each sitting Cézanne had insisted that Vollard sit as still as an apple. When the painting was finally completed, Vollard asked the painter how he liked it. Cézanne replied, "I only like the white collar on your neck."

Give yourself ample time and do not be disappointed by your early results. You cannot expect your first still life to be good and your tenth one to be a masterpiece. The fun is in the doing; simply handling the paint is a thrilling experience.

AFTER THE STORM   *This palette knife painting, rich in textures, is a dramatic design of action and counter-action in a rugged Connecticut countryside.*

Chapter 6 LANDSCAPE PAINTING OUTDOORS

P AINTING outdoors is an excellent way to develop your powers of observation and your visual memory. Although it is difficult to do large or very finished pictures outdoors, you can gather a lot of useful material by painting directly from nature. You can then return home and build more elaborate compositions from these outdoor sketches.

OUTDOOR EQUIPMENT

I always remember how George Bellows, one of America's great painters, prepared for outdoor painting. At the time, early in the twenties, he was experimenting with the so-called "Marratta Color System": a system of pre-mixed tube colors arranged in sets of color harmonies. One harmony, for example, ranged from green to purple with various stages in between; another harmony ranged from blue to red, light to dark. In order to transport all these paints (a hundred or more large tubes), he strapped a wheelbarrow to his car and drove out into the landscape, looking not for a particular scene, but for a fine large shade tree. When he found the tree, he would pile the colors, palette, brushes, and other paraphernalia into the wheelbarrow and wheel this through the meadow to the tree. Then he would study the landscape from every direction, selecting a subject that fitted his mood and choosing the most appropriate color harmony.

Naturally, I do not propose that you set up a system as elaborate as

87

George Bellows'. If you are painting under adverse conditions—burdened by a mountain of equipment—you will find it difficult to concentrate and remain enthusiastic about your work. Bring necessary equipment with you and select a comfortable place to work. It may help you to use the following checklist when you gather your outdoor equipment:

Canvas boards or stretched canvas	Insect repellent
Easel	Paint rags
Paint box	Brushes, knives, palette
Two folding chairs	Tube paint, medium, turpentine
Sun shades	View finder
A light hat	

For outdoor work, canvas boards are more practical than stretched canvas. If you prefer to use stretched canvas, however, be sure the sunlight does not strike the back of the canvas. The light coming through the surface would confuse you when you apply the color.

Do not use sunglasses, because they tend to distort the color. Be sure never to leave behind paint rags after you have finished working: animals will be poisoned by them. Nor should you leave behind paint scrapings. Farmers fear and resent painters on their land if these dangerous trails are left behind.

Set up your easel in a quiet, level spot. If you are using your paint box for an easel, set it up on one of your folding chairs; sit on the other chair, and work directly on the panel that fits into your paint box. Sitting on a rock or on the ground can be very tiring after a while.

In the summertime you may prefer to sit in the shade, because this is the time when the rays of the sun, falling on your painting, strain your eyes and the heat becomes unbearable. Sun shades are less frequently used now than formerly, but they offer good protection when you are painting in hot climates, on a beach, or on a desert. I advise you to bring along a light hat for protection. Examine the ground, particularly for ants and poison ivy, and take along some insect repellent just in case. These are little things to remember; they should not frighten you.

Be sure to watch the tide at the seashore, if you are painting from a rock. The tide can be treacherous. At times I have found myself in a dangerous position because I was too absorbed to notice the rising tide.

CHOOSING YOUR SUBJECT

Many beginners, gazing over a vast panorama of scenery, are plagued by the question, "What shall I paint?" The answer is very simple: begin with the

WHEAT HARVEST, LANCASTER COUNTY   *I completed this painting on a hot, humid July week-end. The leaden sky, contrasting with the golden wheat, and the rich green foliage at the left, lend a richness to the painting, and intensify the mood of an impending storm. (Pennsylvania Collection, Gimbels, Philadelphia, courtesy National Geographic Society)*

89

scenes nearest you; paint the subjects you know and have seen many times. All nature is paintable: a view from your window, the park, a city street, the open country, the mountains, or the sea. Even the same subjects can be painted over and over in many variations, in different weather, under different light, at a different time of day. There are also great seasonal changes from spring to winter, which strongly affect the subject.

Find a quiet place where you are not disturbed by onlookers. A busy city scene may be too crowded and distracting. In the beginning, select a simple subject, perhaps a barn and tree set against the sky. Put away the notion that to paint a great picture you must paint a glamorous subject. Although some great pictures *are* painted of spectacular subjects, their greatness does not depend on the subject alone, but on the artist's skill and interpretation. Any humble scene, well painted, is a greater picture than any glamorous subject badly painted.

The painter I just mentioned, George Bellows, supports exactly this point: it is not the subject itself, but how the subject is *seen* and *treated*, that makes a painting good, bad, or indifferent. Learn how to paint, but, even more important, learn how to *see*. For this reason, do not be overselective when you search for subject matter.

If you are not sympathetic to a subject, do not even consider painting it. You will concentrate more on a scene that appeals to you.

Your subject may seem unexciting at first, but you may find that the deeper you go into it, the more absorbing and exciting the subject becomes. There is always a challenge in painting a simple subject from nature, transforming it into a work of art. Experience will teach you that the more you paint, the more subjects you *want* to paint; you will see things around you that you never saw before. Most people take nature for granted, without ever really seeing it. Most people never study the nature around them, unless the view is extraordinary, like a brilliant autumn foliage, Niagara Falls, or the Grand Canyon.

How many times friends have said to me, "You should have been there to see that sunset—what a picture you would have painted of it!" It seems strange to the layman that artists not only seldom paint such spectacular subjects, but that artists actually have formed an *aversion* to spectacles. Yes, I too like the Grand Canyon, but I have no desire to paint it, because a picture frame could hardly contain a subject so grandiose in detail and color. Since the artist's mission is not to copy nature, this subject is better left to the color photographer.

There *is* a school of painting called *naturalistic* painting which attempts to copy nature, but I find their work very dull and tiring, precisely because what they attempt to do cannot be done! It is impossible to paint every leaf

90

on a tree, every blade of grass in the meadow, and impossible even to give the *appearance* of such detail. The eye refuses to submit to such a factual interpretation of nature.

INTERPRETING THE SUBJECT

The artist interprets nature through color and form, and creates harmony by accenting the essential elements. The painting, so created, becomes a thing in itself; it becomes his personal comment on what he has seen and felt, and the pleasure he has derived from the handling of the paint. The artist's excitement and pleasure are transferred to the onlooker, who, in turn, enjoys the *painting*, rather than the scene painted. Any accidental detail in nature which clouds the artist's statement should be omitted.

When you paint, try to remember what *first* attracted you to the scene, and keep this impression in mind the entire time. Reminding yourself in this way, you will find that your original impression was quite simple: you saw several large shapes juxtaposed and you saw the broad, basic colors. The details did not crowd into your first vision of the scene. This fact is very difficult to remember, because when you start to delineate the scene before you, the scattered, small forms may crop up from nowhere to confuse you; if you arbitrarily paint them, the details will also confuse your picture.

Let us assume you are painting a meadow with bushes and small cedars scattered about, and you consider this foliage essential to the scene. You cannot paint all the bushes and cedars, but you can select a minimum number and place them on the canvas according to the compositional effect you want to achieve. Stick to the main motif, as you first saw it, without being overwhelmed by the accidents of nature. Some of these accidents make excellent pictures, but if you use them, be sure you know why and can bring out their most essential qualities.

Above all, a landscape has a mood. In fact, frequently you will be attracted to the mood alone. You may pass the same place many times and find no interest in painting it, until one day, you see it magically transformed by light and atmosphere, creating an exciting subject for painting.

Bring out the specific qualities of the subject and its mood. Do not search for subjects you remember having seen in other paintings. This kind of imitation should always be avoided, especially in outdoor sketching.

OIL SKETCHES FROM NATURE

You cannot be an effective landscape painter unless you have had long experience sketching nature in its very complex, forever changing moods, lights,

LOW TIDE AT NOON   *This fishing vessel is lying on dry bottom
at low tide. The sun beating straight down produces a colorful
glint in the sand, water, and exposed sea grasses. The old
wreck in the foreground is witness to the ancient fishing
tradition in New England.*

and color effects. Making oil sketches from nature is an exhilarating and absorbing experience.

These oil sketches are like exercises for interpreting and painting nature. Before you attempt to paint the more elaborate, composed landscapes, practice by sketching whatever you see around you. If these sketches sometimes look fragmentary, do not be discouraged; in fact, *avoid* over-finishing them as pictures; rather, concentrate on expressing a clear vision with vitality.

Make your first studies in a medium sized sketchbook, with a soft pencil, before you move onto the canvas. Free of detail, these sketches emphasize the larger shapes, the strong light and shadow, and the modeling of the forms. Take note of the light source and its direction, since all shapes in landscape share the same light and all the shadows fall in the same direction. From these preliminary sketches, select the best composition and design your picture from it.

COMPOSING YOUR SUBJECT

When you set up your canvas outside, you will see a great panoramic view, but obviously you can only paint a fraction of the immensity around you. Study the shape and color relationships of the objects to determine a good pictorial composition. With your view finder (a rectangular opening cut into a three-by-five inch square piece of cardboard), you can isolate sections of the panorama, studying fragments for their compositional interest.

Decide the horizontal and vertical limits you wish to impose on your composition: how much sky and how much foreground. You will seldom find a composition ready-made. Even when you sketch outdoors, feel free to recompose, to eliminate, or to add to your subject. In the preliminary drawings, make the changes that you think would help the composition of the final painting: you may wish to add a vertical direction to the many horizontal lines in your landscape, or you may incorporate a tree or another nearby object into your composition.

It is worth noting that you cannot simply paint the distant mountains without painting a foreground, because it is the foreground that *makes* the mountains look distant. Nor should the mountains be the most distant plane in your picture, touching the upper edge of the frame. There should be enough sky to carry the eye beyond the mountains and yet enough *foreground* to balance the distance.

I do not mean to say that the dividing line between sky and landscape should be in the middle of your canvas. As you remember from Chapter Four, a central dividing line makes it difficult for the eye to move freely from one space to another. Nor should the largest object in your picture be placed in the dead center. You may have to balance a large object on one side of the canvas with another object on the opposite side, or perhaps with a strong cloud formation at the upper portion of the canvas.

Your main decorative motif may be a large group of trees in the middle distance. To give full effect to this motif, you must keep both foreground and distant shapes small. I use this as an example, because it illustrates the point I have made several times; namely, that there are no hard and fast rules in art. You must develop your own picture sense and your own eye for motif and composition. Your sense of balance and design will be your guide.

With charcoal, draw the subject on your canvas; then, using a small brush, go over these lines with cobalt blue thinned with turpentine. I recommend cobalt blue because it adds airiness to your painting. On a gray day, when you use only a little blue in your painting, substitute yellow ochre for the blue.

After completing your oil drawing, dust off the charcoal, because the charcoal substance may gray the colors you apply later. You now have your composition laid in, so relax for a moment. Study the subject you are about to paint and compare it with your lay-in. You may want to improve the composition. Get into the mood of the subject and interpret this mood in your painting. Now you are ready to lay out the colors on your palette.

LAYING IN THE COLORS

Begin by selecting only those colors your subject will require, restricting the palette to a few colors. Remember, you can always add other pigments as the need for them arises. At this time, be sure to squeeze out a good quantity of each color, and twice as much white, because it is very disturbing to stop every ten minutes to find the tubes in your box and squeeze out dabs of color. Put some turpentine in one of the tin cups, and put painting medium in the other, as I suggested in Chapter One. Clean your brushes in turpentine frequently, or whenever they gray out from too much color mixing, and be sure to dry the brush well with paint rags, or the turpentine will dilute your paint too much. Use the paint medium very sparingly or not at all, especially on a hot day when the paint is exceptionally fluid on your palette.

The artist divides landscape space into three planes: foreground, middle distance, and distance. Naturally, there are many intermediary planes, but to avoid confusion, think of landscapes as divided into only three planes. Since the foreground is superimposed on the distant and middle distant planes, start painting the sky and work forward to the foreground.

As you lay in the sky, notice that the light coming from the sky often creates the mood of the entire scene. Observe the variations and densities of

WINTER EVENING   *A luminous night scene of a typical Pennsylvania Dutch village. I painted with a palette knife in rich impasto, using strong color contrasts to bring out the textures and luminosity of the subject. (Collection, Abbott Laboratories)*

95

THE BRIDGE *This painting combines the basic principles of perspective, spatial relationship, color relationship, and design. I kept detail to a minimum, making the shapes themselves speak significantly.*

96

blue, and the volume, movement, and direction of the clouds. Notice that the higher the sky, the darker the blue, producing a dome-like effect over the scene. On the horizon, a clear sky will be pale and pinkish, a color you can achieve by adding white, some cadmium red light, and sometimes even yellow to the blue. This makes the sky appear very atmospheric. Blue, alone, can be terribly hard and cold, especially when you paint a large sky, so modify the blues with inter-mixtures of greens, cadmium reds and yellows, or burnt siennas, without graying the colors too much or making the sky too heavy. The sky should be luminous in relation to the landscape.

After the sky is laid in, paint the distant hills and plains, maintaining a smooth paint texture to simulate the atmospheric effect. Then begin to lay in the larger shapes, their light and dark patterns modeling the forms simply. Roughly indicate textures with thicker and thinner paint applications. Experiment with your brush stroke to bring out volume and form: a long brush stroke will flatten out the form of objects; a short brush stroke will give greater volume to the object. Without being afraid to exaggerate, keep a good contrast of warm and cool colors, light and dark. You will learn how to use these contrasts better after you have seen your sketches indoors. Your sketches may look alive as long as you are outdoors, but they must retain that life away from nature, in the studio.

As you approach the foreground in the painting, increase the body and texture of your paint, as well as the color intensity, creating a color perspective independent of line and plane. Using medium sized and large brushes, keep detail at a minimum. Remember, this is a sketch, not a finished picture, and therefore it should give a vivid short-hand impression of the subject.

During this painting session, take frequent rests: walk around, get your eyes off the picture. When your eyes feel rested, summarize your progress and develop the sketch further. If you look at a subject too long, you lose the feel of color gradations and the distant atmospheric effect. Particularly in landscape painting, your associations and logic will dull your vision; the detail will overwhelm you. A tree in the distance will appear as green as a tree in the foreground and the subtle, atmospheric blue-gray effect on nearby hills will disappear; in short, your picture will look factual and colorless when you see it indoors.

As I mentioned before, I would advise you to limit your painting time to two or, at most, three hours: in that time, the light changes so much that if you continue to paint, you will confuse the picture plane, and probably tire from the intense concentration.

I advise my students to look, every now and then, at the landscape upside down. Bend over until your head is between your legs and take a quick glance, not at the shapes, but only at the color of the objects. You will be surprised by the great contrasts in color, and you can clearly see how the atmosphere and light transform the color and values in the distance.

There is an old saying, "You can't see the forest for the trees." For most beginners, this saying might be even further elaborated by, "You can't see the trees for the leaves." It is obviously impossible to paint every leaf on a tree and each blade of grass in the meadow. In most instances, one cannot see any individual leaves, even at a short distance. Moreover, the slightest breeze puts the leaves in motion and, instead of individual leaf designs, you see only the blurred, larger shapes of the branches and tree.

PAINTING LANDSCAPE TEXTURES

In landscape painting, textures should be particularly well observed and interpreted. Study the density of foliage and clouds, the transparency of sky and water, the coarseness of rocks, the depth and softness of grasses in the meadow, and the depth and texture of the wheat field. Building materials have their own textures, from smooth to rough. Textural effects are produced by applying thicker and thinner, smoother and rougher layers of paint.

Attempt to interpret these textures and forms in shadow, light, and color. The individuality of the tree will appear through its general shape and color, not through its leaves. In a large wooded section containing different kinds of trees, the general shape and color of each type should be indicated in your picture, creating variety and interesting designs: the elm tree is quite different from the maple; the pine is different from the hemlock. In the very foreground, branches can show individual leaves, but only in their *general* character, to differentiate one kind of tree from another.

The textures of fields and meadows are like fur; the thickness and density of grasses differ. Note these differences. Paint the textures (not the detail), applying the paint roughly or smoothly. The textures in the foreground are stronger, gradually diminishing as the distance increases. Foreground textures can be built up with the palette knife; this will give the illusion of depth to your landscape. This aerial perspective can be further enhanced by the gradation of color (see Chapter Four on perspective).

When painting in bright sunlight, keep your color key high (light and bright) and your contrasts great, because the picture will look darker in an indoor light. Always keep your color mixtures fresh and do not over-mix them.

COMPLETING YOUR SKETCH

After you have covered your surface, you may still wish to make changes here and there. Scrape out sections with the palette knife and repaint them, or set in new colors altogether. When setting in new colors, try not to disturb the layer of color below too much; do not use a broad stroke, because it might blur the form. Rather, paint with small, deft strokes of solid pigment. If you wish to make changes at home, let the picture dry first, then make the changes afterwards.

I find that if I put sketches away for several days without looking at them during that time, I am often surprised when I see them again. They have a vitality I had forgotten and they restore the vivid impression of the subject, refreshing my mind and clearing my judgment. I leave this up to you: sometimes it is better to start work on a painting as soon as you return to your studio; sometimes it helps to set the sketch aside for a few days to clear your mind.

When the sketch is thoroughly dry, brush the surface with a thin coat of retouching varnish to restore the original freshness of the color. Avoid later repainting and finishing: the charm of the sketch is in its freshness.

SAINT PATRICK'S CATHEDRAL *This painting contrasts the old and new styles of architecture. I divided the color patterns sharply for contrast.*

Chapter 7 LANDSCAPE PAINTING
IN THE STUDIO

B Y PAINTING landscapes in the studio, you can concentrate on the elements of nature that change constantly: light, texture, cloud formations, aerial perspective. Studio painting refines your knowledge of landscape painting and gives you time to undertake far more ambitious landscapes than are possible outdoors.

USING YOUR SKETCHES

With a good background in sketching from nature, you will develop a memory that helps greatly when you work indoors. When you see a subject you like, make a number of compositional drawings from nature to suggest the total effect of the scene. You might write in the names of the colors in the scene and draw certain details you wish to incorporate, such as animals, people, architectural detail, or trees in the foreground. Using the color sketches you made on the spot, you are ready to work in your studio.

After making my studies, I go directly to my studio and start painting without delay. Landscape subjects transform every day and you may not be able to return to them to refresh your memory. They have to be in your mind completely before you start to paint.

UNION SQUARE   *This is an airy picture with a minimum of detail.*
With the palette knife, I painted in contrasting cool and warm optical
grays, enriched by the greens of the trees and grass. The movement
of the people and pigeons adds a liveliness to the scene.

102

USING OTHER AIDS IN THE STUDIO

Some students copy the work of other artists, an activity which has some value, provided that you select works by the masters. Copying provides an understanding of composition and of interpreting nature. You can learn how to formalize and how to create unity in a picture.

Some students work from photographs in the studio. After you have had some experience sketching from nature, you will see that the photograph tends to distort perspectives and flatten volumes. Foreground objects appear too large and distant objects too small, fading away. The photograph records all of the accidental surface detail, an effect which would destroy the unity in a painting.

The photograph, however, is very valuable to technical artists, illustrators, and mural painters. They have learned how to use photographs for accurate mechanical detail, or for painting actions that are too fast for the eye to see. I would not advise the beginner to use photographs until he is well acquainted with the visual world by sketching directly from nature.

In short, I think it is wisest to use the preparatory sketches you made on the spot.

DRAWING IN THE COMPOSITION

Start with the design of your composition on your canvas. Make the initial drawing in charcoal and feel free to make changes. If you need a vertical line, draw in a tree or a house or any other object, even though it was not in the actual scene. You may wish to enlarge the mountains, add or eliminate clouds, or change the color scheme. Remember, you create your own reality in your picture.

LAYING IN THE COLORS

After the drawing is completed and the charcoal sprayed with fixative, lay in your colors in broad, rich strokes of oil paint. Start painting the sky and work toward the foreground, maintaining an atmospheric effect, and keeping the edges soft.

When laying in your picture, keep the colors bright and varied in hue, and in cool and warm sensation. Generally, when the light area of the form is warm, the shaded area of the form will be cool; likewise, when the light plane is cool, the form is warm in the shaded area. For example, a red apple is obviously warm on the side that faces the light, but cool on the shadow side; conversely, a green apple is cool on the side that faces the light, but warm on the shadow side. The sunlight falling on a white house produces yellow-white (warm) in the light planes, while the shaded planes show blue-violet (cool). The shadowed side of a *blue* house, on the other hand, consists of *warm* blue-grays, while the light planes are *cool*.

PAINTING SKY AND CLOUDS

The sky is like an overhead dome. On a clear day, the sky tends toward warm yellow or pink blue on the horizon, gradually darkening, cooling, becoming blue as it rises higher. Clouds form a kind of ceiling over the scene: a dark cool plane shows *beneath* the clouds; lighter, warmer colors appear on the edges and *above* the clouds. Clouds are generally thick masses of vapor except in extremely thin sections; study their volume, and design them to move with the rhythm of your landscape.

The variety of cloud shapes produces a variety of effects on the sky and landscape. For example, between dense storm clouds there may be openings in the sky where the sun or light rays come through. Sometimes the darkest clouds, floating just over the hills, make the hills appear lighter by contrast. Some clouds throw heavy shadows on the hills, making the slopes appear deep blue and purple against the lighter distant sky. Observe these moods well: they are an asset to your landscape.

PAINTING WATER

Many beginners are puzzled when they try to paint water, a subject which you can learn to paint by observing its rhythm, color, and texture. As you watch from the shore, waves move forward in rapid succession, breaking and disappearing before you have time to study their shapes and movements. If you watch them for a while, you will begin to notice that their movement and size repeat every now and then. Studying this repetition helps you understand the movement and design of waves.

A pool of still water or a calm lake on a windless day resembles a mirror by reflecting, in reverse, the objects on the shore, the sky, and clouds. The colors in the reflection are subdued, grayer and greener than the objects themselves, and sometimes tinted with brown or blue. Naturally, a slight wind will distort these reflections, and a stronger wind will agitate the surface even more, breaking the reflections into small fragments. If there is too much agitation, there will be no reflection on the surface of the water at all.

Although a river in motion does not reflect any objects, the *color* of the water changes according to the colors of the sky and the light. Observe the ocean and distant lakes and notice how the color of the sky and light

STEP 1   *I established the composition of this picture with a charcoal drawing on the canvas. At this stage, I concerned myself with the distribution of spaces, the action and counter-action of the vertical, horizontal, and diagonal lines. I made the detail and compositional pencil sketches on the spot and painted the picture later in my studio. I eliminated much of the detail to emphasize the overall mood of this scene.*

STEP 2 *After I sprayed the charcoal drawing with fixative, I began to lay in the sky with oil paint, using thalo blue, white, viridian, and black. In order to achieve a rich and agitated texture, I applied the paint with my painting knife. Note how the sky creates the general mood of the landscape. I felt that the agitated, dark sky and the old gnarled trees emphasized the feeling of the new, untrodden snow, and the classical simplicity of the early New England church.*

106

STEP 3   *After I established the general mood of the sky, I laid in the planes of the church and snow. I kept the contrast of light and dark to a minimum, because there was no direct sunlight. I used the palette knife to simulate the smooth surface of the new snow. I then laid in the larger shapes of the trees, as well as the windows of the church, using cadmium yellow pale, yellow ochre, burnt sienna, and venetian red, grayed with thalo blue. Detail is kept to a minimum!*

107

STEP 4   *In this final stage, I developed the texture of the sky and
the trees. The architectural details of the church, shutters and
windows were added, as well as the smaller branches of the trees
and shrubbery. I used a four-inch painting knife for the entire
painting, and a number eight sable brush for the sharp detail of
the architecture and branches. I used no paint medium, except
in the rendering of the final detail.* (NEW SNOW, *Collection,
Metropolitan Museum of Art, courtesy American Artists Group*)

108

affect the color of the water. As a general rule, when water is light on the horizon, it will darken as it comes toward you; conversely, when the water is dark on the horizon, it will lighten as it comes toward you. Not only the intensity, but the hue of the color changes with atmospheric and light conditions. The water appears blue or green on a sunny day, gray on a cloudy day, and pink at sunset.

PAINTING SHADOWS

Light does not exist in a picture without shadow. Here is the first principle of light and shadow: since light comes from one direction, the shadows must all fall uniformly in the opposite direction. For this reason, it is important to organize your shadows well.

The shadow of the house will not fall in a different direction from the shadow of the tree next to it. The shadows of distant trees, hills, and mountains all fall in the same direction.

Strong sun throws very strong shadows, obvious to everyone. But even on a gray day, you can perceive the shadows under forms. These shadows add softness to the objects and tie the forms together, creating unity in the picture. The strong shadows in sunlight accentuate the forms, but they should never be too dark or they will create holes in your picture. When the direction of shadows is not well controlled, the picture looks confused.

The second principle of light and shadow is this: cast shadows follow the contour of the land and the contour of all the shapes on which the shadows fall. The shadows on grass have rough, ragged edges because of the irregularity of the grass. Shadows on a smooth road, however, show clean edges, defining precisely the shape of the object that is casting the shadow. On hilly or uneven ground, always make your shadows follow the irregular contour. A flat shadow will never fall on a deeply plowed field.

Here we must differentiate between the shadow plane *on* the object and shadows *cast* by the object onto another surface. The shadows *on* an object, whether the object is a tree or a face, are handled in the way I described in the chapter on still life painting. Shadows on hills are similar to shadows on fruit: the shadow accentuates the volume of the hill, just as the shadow accentuates the volume of the apple. In painting shadows on trees, on landscape objects in general, be sure that the textures are not lost by an over-emphasis on shadow edges.

Keep the edges of *cast* shadows soft, as well, indicating the density or texture of the terrain on which they are falling. One thing you should always remember: cast shadows should not be as important as the objects which cast them.

A dense tree throws a dense shadow; a sparse tree shows perforated patterns in its shadows. Mornings and evenings, when the sun is low on the horizon, the light is directed at an oblique angle and the shadows tend to be elongated, but not intense. At high noon, the shadows tend to be most intense and dark, falling directly under the object.

Often clouds throw large shadows over a section of landscape, an effect which can be very useful in landscape painting. The weight and darkness of these shadows depend on the thickness and density of the clouds. Cloud shadows can frequently be used as a compositional device to mask sections of a landscape, or to add color and movement to an otherwise monotonous landscape. A large stretch of yellow brown on the Arizona desert, for example, will not give any relief to the eye unless cloud shadows play over the desert, with their contrasting colors of blue and violet.

In addition to the density and shape of the shadow, also observe its color. For example, at a distance, shadows become softer and bluer. Delacroix, one of the great French painters of the nineteenth century, describes an experience he had. One day, as he was coming out of the dimly lit Louvre Museum, he noticed a carriage with a white horse, standing on the yellow, sandy street. Delacroix was startled to discover that the shadow looked *pure violet*. This was a revelation which profoundly influenced his work.

PAINTING SNOW

Snow is a fascinating and very popular subject for painters. I have painted many snow scenes. The silence of the landscape blanketed by a gentle snowfall has a greater appeal to me than a dramatic colorful interpretation of the same subject. I interpret the scene with clear grays and whites, enriching these colors with a deep, tonal sky. Contrasting the snow with umber tones, blacks, and greens, I produce an effect of cool and warm opposition.

I also contrast whites with one another, particularly the whites in buildings, because they take on such different color casts. A church, newly painted, looked pure white to me before the snow came, but after a snowfall, the white was transformed into a greenish, yellowish cast. These are very interesting nuances of close color harmonies which, in an apparently white-gray picture, are colorful and pleasing to the eye.

White from the tube has little relation to the magical white of snow. In fact, pure white can rarely be used effectively in snow scenes, even in the brightest planes. In pictures without sunlight, I mix various tones of white, black, and viridian green to obtain the color for snow, a color which produces a soft and cool effect, as well as a warm quality on the buildings.

Delineate the thickness of the blanket of snow and notice that the

HEMISPHERES AT BATON ROUGE   *Industrial subjects, seen in the right kind of light, can be very dramatic. I made many drawings at night when the light and dark enveloped much of the detail. The artificial light added life to the subject. (Collection, Massachusetts Institute of Technology)*

LOBSTERMEN'S SHACKS, MONHEGAN ISLAND   *This is a rustic, but colorful, subject consisting of buildings, floats, traps, and boats in the harbor of Monhegan. I painted the picture with a palette knife, using sketches I had made on location.*

112

deeper the snow, the softer the shapes covered by the snow. Sometimes the contours make grotesque shapes. The branches of trees are thickly laden, while the snow clings only spottily to the tree trunks. Observe the thickness of snow on rooftops particularly. If you just paint white lines over the roof, your picture will look thin and unconvincing. Generally, on a snow-covered roof, the top plane is light, and the edge plane is grayer, showing depth.

Yellow grasses and thin brush lines add a fine tracery and textural effect to the snow picture. The depth of foot prints and car tracks should also be well delineated.

PAINTING DAWN, SUNSETS, AND NOCTURNES

There are many extraordinarily beautiful effects in nature, effects which are frequently independent of the landscape's topography. Light, for example, can transform a common subject into glorious beauty. During the hour before dawn, when the mist rises from the valley, the sky is tinged with violet, yellow, and pale blue; the hills are dark and purple, and there is a muted silence in the air. These effects are momentary. For this reason, they cannot be painted on the spot; I have painted this subject from drawings with written-in color notations. As you observe the transformation of nature, you will develop a retentive memory for color and mood.

Earlier in this book, I mentioned that many artists form an aversion to painting sunsets, because they shy away from the obvious. Beauty, ready-made, does not appeal to them very much. The challenge of painting is in the process of interpreting the *subtle* aspects of nature.

The nineteenth century English painter, Turner, specialized in painting dramatic atmospheric effects in nature: storms at sea, nights in Venice, and sunsets, created entirely from his short notations and small watercolor sketches. Turner's sunsets are glorious, painted in heavily loaded pigments, achieving a transparency of light that has never been rivaled. Every inch of Turner's canvas is permeated by color, and yet the reality of the scene is so great that one feels enveloped by the painting. One may wonder, did Turner *really* see these things, or did he study nature so long that he *imagined* these fleeting moments of glory? When a dowager visited his studio at the height of his fame, Turner showed her a sunset painting. The lady said, "But, Mr. Turner, I have never seen such a sunset before!" To which Turner replied, "Don't you wish you *had?*"

Night scenes (nocturnes) have great fascination for painters. Nocturnes convey a special mood. I have painted many night views of New York, its towering buildings and glittering lights. A common scene can be magically transformed at nightfall, bathed in mysterious colors, producing strange moods.

DRIFTWOOD, MONHEGAN ISLAND   *This sunset scene is enveloped by a salmon pink atmosphere. The tree trunks, mauled by the sea, have a rough surface. The black rocks and white surf and spray produce a dynamic effect.*

Chapter 8 VARIATIONS ON
A THEME

114

I N THE preceding chapters on landscape painting, I discussed basic techniques in order to provide a general approach to the subject. Now I
should like to go a step further by demonstrating how a simple motif can
be transformed into greater significance through a number of variations.

PAINTING THE FIRST VERSION

Some years ago, in Maine, I sketched the wreck of a little fishing boat.
Around the wreck were scattered rotten fishing nets, ropes, seaweed, and
driftwood, on a gentle terrain. This was not a particularly exciting subject
for me, and I thought no more about it until I returned to my studio in
Connecticut a few days later. I brought out the sketch, along with some
other drawings I had made on my trip, and I realized that the scene was a
subject with great potential: the sea, the creek, the breakwater, and the
wreck lying in the sunlight could be composed nicely. I decided to make a
painting of it.

Although I had made only a few color notes of the wreck, my mind was
filled with the vision of the many nuances of color so typical of that region
in Maine.

The painting, "The Wreck at Turbot's Creek," resulted from my quick
pencil sketch. With few changes, the wreck is just as it appeared the day I
sketched it in Maine.

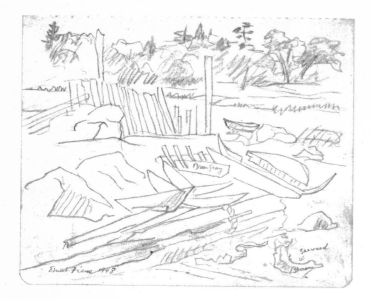

When I was in Maine, I made this quick sketch of a wreck, its remnants cast off on a desolate beach. The sketch is very rough, containing only a few simple color notations, and a general suggestion of the scene.

VARIATION #1

As I studied the finished painting, I realized that the subject could be made more dramatic and more significant if I accentuated the relationship of the wreck to the ocean. I began to work immediately on a variation of the realistic original. Instead of a gentle, sunny day, I painted a stormy day. I redesigned the composition, replacing the trees in the middle ground with a small rocky island, and placing the wreck directly on the ocean shore. I painted the wreck in roughly the same position as I did the original version, but the design is simpler. I eliminated many details—the creek, for example. I emphasized the ocean, the movement of the breakwater, and the dark clouds to convey the stormy feeling I wanted. The long pole running from the edge of the water to the cloud stabilizes the composition, tying the various elements together.

Note that all the major lines are conceived more dynamically than in the first, more realistic picture. The color is deeper and more sonorous; the thrust is stronger, contributing to the dramatic, vital effect of this version.

Painting a series was not my original intention, but as I studied the first two paintings, I felt that the subject had still greater design possibilities. It also occurred to me that the structure of this wreck resembled the bone structure of a fish: an interesting symbol of the sea.

116

THE WRECK AT TURBOT'S CREEK   *At the studio, I painted the scene,*
remaining fairly true to the sketch: a realistic version of the wreck.

117

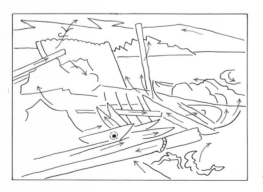

VARIATION #1 *I redesigned the first composition and painted a new version of the wreck, dramatizing its relationship to the stormy ocean. I reduced the detail, and accentuated the broad movement of the sky and water. The pole, running from the shore to the sky, stabilizes the composition. Notice how I accentuated the thrusts and counter-thrusts in this version. (Collection, Art Students League of New York)*

Schematic Drawing for Variation #1

I painted a series of experimental casein sketches, transforming the wreck structure and debris into larger designs, under different conditions and from different angles. From many casein studies, I selected the most significant ones and developed them into a series of paintings. I have diagrammed each picture to help you see the compositional variations.

VARIATION #2

In this second variation, I further explored the design quality of the wreck. Viewed in a more two-dimensional manner, the painting de-emphasizes the element of depth. The fish-like structure of the wreck is now plain. I painted the wreck in approximately the same location again, but I separated and enlarged the fragments to emphasize the composition and to create an interesting design.

I painted the background sand salmon pink, and contrasted this color with a large section of chartreuse yellow in the boards. The cross sections of the boat structures are gray and black. I painted the background in deeper colors: dark sky and dark blue ocean. By simplifying and enlarging the rock formations, and by designing the patterns in the sand and foreground into lighter and darker sections of overlapping planes, I added interest to the entire composition.

VARIATION #3

This third variation is the most dramatic of the series—a complete transformation. The day is very stormy; the water is crashing against the shore, driving the wreck inward. I reversed the position of the wreck in order to direct the thrust toward the shore. I retained only the most essential timbers of the boat, creating a flaring design which casts the movement toward the lower left corner of the picture. This strong diagonal movement is counter-balanced by the diagonal thrust of the three cliffs, running from the upper left corner to the lower right. The bow of the boat (resembling a fish head) accentuates the inward movement, a movement which is further emphasized by the part of a torn sail.

The deep purple rocks continue the agitation of the whole scene. The wreck itself is black. The violet, gray, and yellow-white sky complement the strong yellow and white sand of the foreground.

Note that the patterns of the rocks and sky are accentuated by sharp linear strokes. This accentuation produces a dramatic effect, yet retains the stability of the composition.

VARIATION #2   *More abstract than the first versions, this*
painting emphasizes the fish-like structure of the wreck. In
order to stress the design, I deliberately flattened the dimensions
and separated and enlarged the fragments of the wreck.
(Collection, Whitney Museum of American Art)

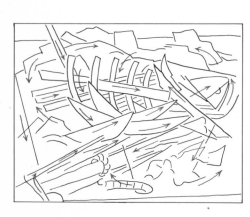

Schematic Drawing for Variation #2

VARIATION #3   *Placed in exactly the opposite direction, the
wreck in this version becomes a dynamic, dramatic victim
of a storm. The sharp, linear strokes of the sky, rocks, and
wreck promote an agitated, almost frenzied, movement in the
painting. I greatly reduced the details of the wreck and created
a sharp tension of movements. I accentuated the movement
of the wreck toward the ocean by repeating the design of the
hull's rib structures. I pulled the movement back to the shore
by painting a torn sail and fish-head bow at the left hand
corner, and by painting waves moving inward. (Collection,
Nelson A. Rockefeller)*

Schematic Drawing for Variation #3

121

VARIATION #4

In the fourth variation, the storm has subsided and the wreck is now rolling onto the shore. To emphasize the billowing movement, I juxtaposed the various parts of the wreck itself. I designed the ribs of the hull to heighten this rolling effect. The entire complex design of the wreckage is silhouetted sharply against the white breakers curling in toward shore.

The marginal design—along the edge of the canvas—ties in the movement and repeats the design rhythm, at the same time.

The water is green, the sky is pale blue and pink. The shore and red rocks are bathed in sunlight.

VARIATION #5

In the fifth variation, the wreck is in repose, lying in soft, rich, golden yellow sand. I shifted the setting from the stark Maine coast to the Caribbean Sea, rendering a calm, restful effect. In this version, the fish symbol is even more emphasized than in any other picture of the series.

I painted the wreck in glowing coral and gray, with black accents. The sky is light blue and pink, with dark cloud formations to the right. To heighten the texture of the water, I painted pure black over an ultramarine blue underpainting. Again, I used an outside marginal design—painted this time in gray-white and gray-pink. The rock formations are deep mauve and red. By holding the diminishing perspective to a minimum, I maintained the two-dimensional plane of the picture surface.

VARIATION #6

In the sixth variation, I juxtaposed the black wreck against one of the great stark rock formations on the Maine Coast: Baldhead Cliff. Because of the complex background, I used only the few largest elements of the wreck, placing all of this massive weight against a pale blue sky. The painting is a design of motion and counter-motion; the composition emphasizes vertical, horizontal, and diagonal movements, thrust and counter-thrust. The foreground rock formations balance the objects in the middle distance.

Note the marginal bands confining this weighty subject, a device I used to give the picture a feeling of airiness.

I painted the huge cliff tan and red, with a large black streak in the center; the water green-blue, with sharp dark-blue accents; and small margins of yellow sand at the bottom of the cliff. The white breakers in the foreground support and unify the whole composition.

VARIATION #4   *No longer the victim of a raging storm, the wreck now reveals a rhythmical, undulating movement, as opposed to the abrupt, linear effects of the last version. Notice how the remnants of the old ship are silhouetted against the white breakers of the ocean, an effect that reinforces the sweeping design. This design is further reinforced by the marginal design at the lower edge of the canvas.*

Schematic Drawing for Variation #4

VARIATION #5   Here I wanted to emphasize a restful motif
in the scene. Without destroying the fish-like structure of the
wreck, I reduced the intense movement of the painting by
placing the wreck on a calm Caribbean shore. Again, I used a
marginal design at the base of the painting to echo the
major motif, and I held the perspective to a minimum.

Schematic Drawing for Variation #5

Schematic Drawing for Variation #6

VARIATION #6 *Here I removed the wreck from the shore
altogether. By placing the remnants in the water, I reduced
the magnitude of the wreck itself. The rigid rock formations
of Maine's Baldhead Cliff produce a complex, weighty design
which I offset by painting airy marginal bands surrounding
the edges of the picture. The white breakers help unify the
composition. (Collection, Alan D. Gruskin)*

VARIATION #7   *Using a vertical composition, I again shifted the setting to the Caribbean. Along the edge of the canvas I painted a marginal design to solidify the composition and to complement the irregular shapes of the wreck. (Collection, Roy R. Neuberger)*

Schematic Drawing for Variation #7

VARIATION #7

The setting for this seventh variation is the Caribbean, just as it was in the fifth variation: the locale lends itself to the basic design quality. The color scheme is composed of golden yellow sand, coral-red rocks, and pink-violet sky. The water is a solid ultramarine blue, with an overlay of pure black giving texture to the water. I completed the design in the foreground by painting pink rocks and a brown seaweed formation. The marginal design at the edge of the canvas (painted in gray with strong black lines) solidifies the composition and complements the irregular shape of the inner subject, adding liveliness to the entire composition. The wreck itself is burnt sienna with black accents, as opposed to the yellow, pink, and black background; and the grain of the wood adds texture to the large elements of the wreck.

This is the last painting of the series. The entire project spanned a period of two years, an exciting experience in developing a theme and abstracting from nature.

The real challenge to the painter is in painting a moving and meaningful picture by communicating his feelings clearly and vividly. You can recreate a scene, make any changes you wish, or transform it entirely. However, your picture must convey a sense of reality to the onlooker. At first, work close to nature; as you mature in your understanding of nature, and in the mastery of your material, you will be able to express yourself with greater freedom and imagination.

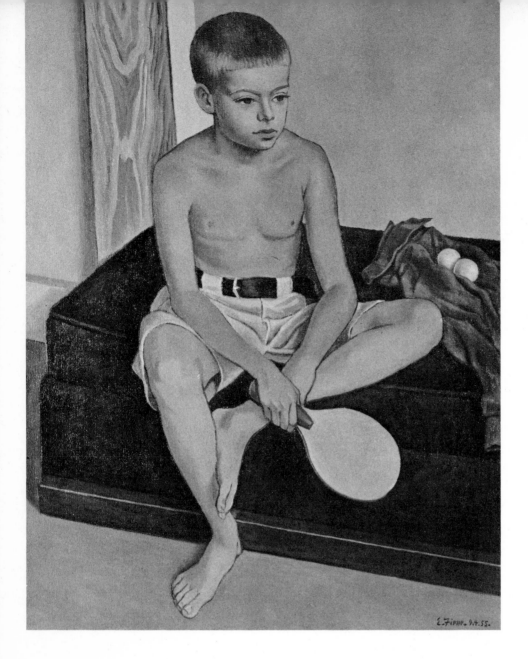

THE PING PONG PLAYER *This painting of my son, Paul, proves that you can find interesting models among your family and friends. Notice the sharp foreshortening of the legs and the relaxed position of the head.*

Chapter 9 FIGURE

PAINTING

T HE HUMAN figure is the most fascinating subject for the artist. In painting the human form, you should have some knowledge of muscular structure and proportion. For this, I suggest you enter a life class where you can draw the nude either in an art school or with some informal group of students.

An able teacher helps a great deal, but if you do not have the opportunity to study with a teacher, there are means of studying on your own. Sketch bathers on a beach; invite friends to pose for you in their bathing suits; draw statues in museums and parks (since they are stationary, you can take all the time you need to study and design the forms). Art students in the Renaissance learned by copying the drawings of their masters. Some present-day educators, who know more about John Dewey's theories than they know about art, take a dim view of this method; but since copying did not inhibit the imagination and creativity of Michelangelo or Rembrandt, I see no reason why I should not recommend this procedure to you.

There are also many magazines containing photographs of figures in a variety of poses and attire; they can serve as models for you. Do not trace or copy the photographs, but try to draw from them as you would draw from a live model. You will soon get the general feel of the figure, its proportions, volume, and the actions of the limbs. Take every opportunity to sketch the people around you. There is nothing more enjoyable or helpful.

PROPORTIONS OF THE FIGURE

The Greeks, with their passion for mathematics and faith in the harmony of numbers, worked out an ideal set of proportions for the human figure. I base my discussion of proportions on the Greek concepts, although the student cannot construct a figure solely by mathematical rules any more than a composer can write a fugue by rules alone. Nevertheless, the principles of proportion should be firmly lodged somewhere in the back of your mind whenever you draw the figure.

The length of the head, from the chin to the top of the skull, is used as the basic measuring unit: the average male figure is seven and one-half heads high; the woman is slightly shorter. The length of the foot is the same as the length of the head. The length of the hand is the length of the face, from chin to hairline. The shoulders are three times the width of the head.

The woman's shoulders are narrower than the man's and her figure is shorter. The male is broad in the shoulders and narrow in the hips; the female is narrow in the shoulders and broad in the hips. The woman's rib cage is smaller in all dimensions; her figure has round, graceful curves and long flowing lines. The male is muscular, showing rugged broken forms, straight and angular lines, and sharply defined planes.

The sizes of children vary according to age: compared to the adult's, a child's head is larger in proportion to the figure. Although each human varies from the norm, the overall difference between figures is slight. A figure that is eight heads high appears to be very tall, one of seven heads is short, but the difference between them is not terribly great.

I do not recommend that you study anatomy in detail. Knowledge of anatomy comes with careful observation as you draw. However, you should own a good book of anatomical diagrams to which you can refer, as a writer refers to his dictionary.

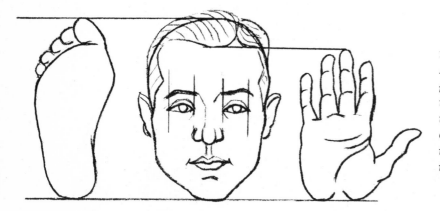

HEAD, FOOT, HAND PROPORTIONS
*According to traditional
principles of proportion,
the foot is the same length as
the head; the hand is the length
of the face from chin to hairline;
the space between the eyes is
the length of one eye.*

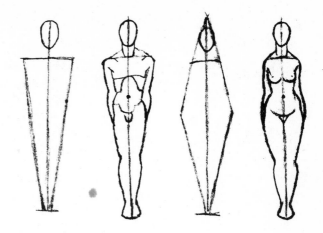

DIFFERENCES IN STRUCTURE
Notice the differences between the male and female bodies: the male's body is broad at the shoulders and narrow at the hips; the female is narrow at the shoulders and broad at the hips.

MEASURING THE FIGURE

The student should not depend too much on mechanical measurement, but should train his eyes to see proportions. Your objective is to make a spontaneous, fluid drawing—an objective which cannot be achieved solely by mechanical means. We use measurement only as a check, when our eye tells us that the drawing seems distorted.

To establish the proportions of your subject, first measure the head since the head is the basic unit. Hold a pencil between your forefinger and thumb, and stretch your arm straight forward, full-length, toward your subject. Closing one eye, line up the head of your subject with the pencil. The length of the head should be between the top of the pencil and the top of your thumb. Holding your thumb in the same place, move this measure from the chin down to the feet, and count how many "heads" are in the body. Remember that your arm must extend straight out for each measurement. Mark each step on the paper. This method of measuring is particularly useful in finding the proportions of foreshortened or seated figures.

THE FIGURE IN ACTION

It is not enough to know merely the proportions and anatomy of the figure. You must also learn the basic rules governing the figure in action. For example, when the weight of a standing figure is shifted to the left foot, the left hip is forced upward. The right leg relaxes, the knee bends, and the right hip falls lower than the left. To maintain balance, the torso and chest swing forward, the right shoulder rises, and the head moves to a position directly over the feet. Just a simple movement like shifting weight will affect every part of the body. A more violent action creates even more exaggerated movements of the head, thorax, and pelvis. Observe your reflection in the mirror as you go through some simple actions.

131

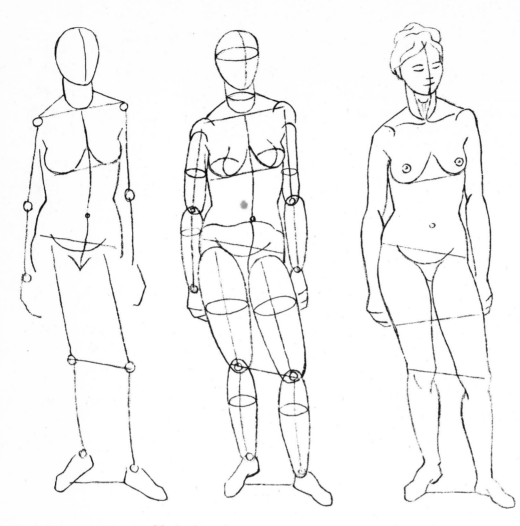

SHIFTING BODY WEIGHT *Notice how the movement
of the entire body is affected by a slight shift in
weight. When the weight is shifted to the right leg,
the left leg relaxes; the right hip thrusts upward and
the left hip drops slightly; the torso and chest swing
forward; the left shoulder rises; the head moves to
a position directly over the feet.*

When one foot is put forward—in walking, for example—the balance of
the whole body changes. The central axis of this movement is the spinal
column. The spinal column can move and twist in all directions, but notice
how differently the limbs move. Using anatomical diagrams, make simplified
drawings of the skeleton to acquaint yourself with its structure. Study the
head, chest, and pelvic section, and notice how the arm and leg bones are
attached.

132

The figure, even in a very relaxed sitting or reclining position, also expresses strong action. You should not only consider what the figure *looks* like, but what it is *doing*. Drawn or painted in this way, the figure will not look like a still life.

USING A MANIKIN

You have seen very realistic dummies in show windows. Since these dummies have no spines, their actions are very limited. The student can find a more realistic dummy, called a *manikin*, at the art material store which can be used for studying the motion of the figure. These manikins are wooden figures, in good proportions, with movable joints; the torso is divided into two sections to simulate the movement of the spine. Manikins come in several models, with round and square structures. The round structures resemble anatomical structure and modeling; the square shapes emphasize volume and flat planes. These manikins make good models for studying both action and foreshortening.

Make drawings from the manikin placed in various positions. Do not attempt to copy the specific shapes of the manikin; simply indicate the larger masses of head and torso. Draw the legs and arms to look like sticks. When you arrange the manikin, be sure that the limbs move rhythmically and that

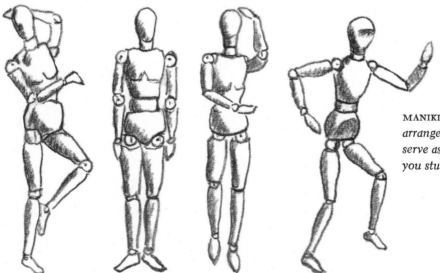

MANIKINS *Wooden manikins, arranged in a variety of positions, serve as excellent models when you study the figure.*

the correct compensations of weight take place. In walking, when the left leg moves forward, the left arm moves backward and the right arm moves forward. These are not accidental movements: they distribute the weight to maintain balance. In running, jumping, climbing, and even in repose, the figure maintains this balance. It may help you to put your manikin into the positions of figures reproduced in newspapers or magazines, particularly in the sports sections.

After having drawn these plain stick figures, you can fill in the head, torso, and limbs. Placed correctly, the lines of the stick figures give action and proportion to the figure. Since the limbs radiate from the torso, it is important to sketch in the head, neck, and torso before you fill in the arms and legs. Add detail and subtle transitions later. Shade these forms in the manner I discussed in the section on shading and value in Chapter Four.

SKETCHING THE MODEL

You can learn a great deal about the figure from drawing. As a preliminary step to painting, this practice will be invaluable to you. You will acquire an understanding of form and proportions, knowledge which should be second nature to you before you face the complexities of painting.

Use a large drawing pad (19″ x 24″) or wrapping paper for these

SKETCHING FROM MANIKINS *As you sketch from the manikin, concentrate on rendering its overall action, making only a rough indication of the limbs and the larger masses of head and torso. Later you can fill in these stick figures.*

sketches. You should not be precious in your work at this stage of the game. Make hundreds of drawings—large and free—and you will soon get into a rhythm of drawing. These rough sketches will teach you how to lay out the figure in action and at rest. Later you can advance to modeling, the head, and figure detail.

While you are drawing the figure, stay a good distance away from the paper. This helps you keep a broader view of the proportions on the sheet. You should make the drawings with soft charcoal, in simple, strong lines; do not worry about making a clean drawing. Using a chamois as an eraser, wipe out sections to make your corrections in the actions and proportions. A clean drawing will come later, when you have gained experience. Working with a pencil would be too restricting at this time, and you would be erasing endlessly, a time-consuming activity.

In these first rough drawings, do not sketch the eyes, nose, mouth, fingers, or toes. Concentrate on the actions, proportions, and the larger forms of the figure. Articulate the joints; show how the pelvis section is related to the thigh; draw the knee joint and the lower leg; show how the shape of the foot relates to the limb. So often beginners draw the pelvis, thigh, lower leg, and foot as one piece, like a cut-out board, flat and meaningless. To understand the mechanism of the human body, draw the separate parts of the body—the shape of the head, the neck, the chest, and abdomen—in a free manner. Doing this will help you develop volume, life, and movement in the figure. The figure is so complex that merely copying what you see before you will not have any clarity or unity. Unless you acquire this general knowledge of the body, you will draw only a conglomeration of detail.

I advise you to draw small shapes larger than you think they actually are. Even then, the shapes may not be large enough. Preconceived notions unconsciously influence you: you may think that beautiful women should have small feet and small hands, for instance. This is not true in reality, and when women are so delineated they look deformed. A woman's head is generally smaller than a man's head; therefore, it follows that a woman's hands and feet are smaller than the man's. They should, however, be drawn in proportion to the rest of the body.

Very often, the beginner draws the neck too long because he has not observed the neck carefully. Notice that the neck overlaps the shoulder line and reaches to the collar bone (clavicle). If the neck line is drawn as though the neck ended at the shoulder line, the head would not fit onto the body properly.

It is difficult for the beginner to see relative proportions while he is drawing. For this reason, I advise you to step back occasionally and observe your work from a distance. Put your drawing on an easel or pin it to the wall and study it from six to eight feet away. In this way, you can see the whole figure, and you will soon find where you went wrong.

FIGURE DISTORTION

It is not the aim of art to reproduce the physical world exactly as it appears. Michelangelo, El Greco, Rubens, and other masters used distortion to suit their artistic objectives. However, they knew so much about the human figure that they could effectively distort it.

When a less knowledgeable artist distorts the figure, the result is often a grotesque failure. In life, you may be repelled by a deformity; how can you accept it in art? Although you intend to heighten the power of the neck, for example, by making it thicker and longer, the result may be a total disfigurement. Any other object—a tree or a rock—may be transformed at will. But if you alter the human figure indiscriminately, you will find that it looks peculiar, even monstrous.

Saying this, I do not mean to imply that the subject for a painting must be the ideal, the most beautiful male or female figure. Far from it. An old, gnarled woman is often a better subject than a sleek, pretty figure. Nature works its own distortions. Beneath the skin, the construction and anatomy of these figures are alike, but time leaves its mark. An old coal miner, having spent most of his life in a bent position, shows a different external physique from an old athlete. Watch for these differences, but do not exaggerate them to distortion.

THE CLOTHED FIGURE

Although the nude will probably be the basis of your figure studies, and possibly the subject of many paintings, you will have more occasion to paint the draped or clothed figure. When you paint the clothed figure, always keep in mind that the body is beneath the clothes and that the folds of the clothing must suggest the form beneath. It was the custom during the Renaissance to draw the nude figure first, and then to clothe it afterward. Whichever way you prefer to work—drawing the nude first or working directly from the clothed figure—the figure underneath must determine the nature of the folds.

Whether you create a figure wearing a loin cloth, a bathing suit, or full dress, the figure itself remains. Drapery hangs from the point at which it is held; it follows the form and then hangs free. Drapery fits tightly around the flexed joint, falling, rhythmically in folds of varied patterns. In the tension and suspension of clothing, the figure, although modified, is still apparent.

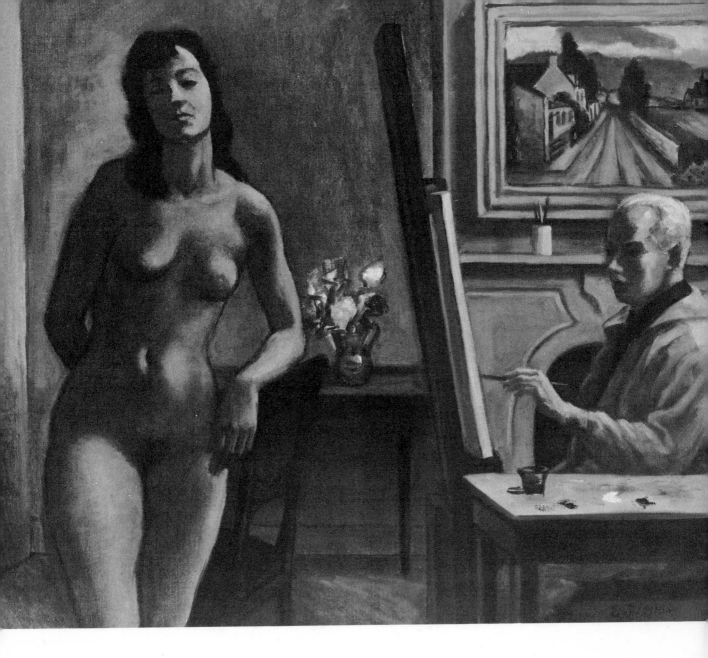

THE ARTIST AND THE MODEL   *I painted this studio view from a reflection in a large mirror. Everything is in reverse; notice that the right hand appears as the left hand. You see this kind of reversal whenever the artist has used a single mirror in a self portrait.*

137

GLASSBLOWER QUINTET II   *Glassblowing requires fast-moving
teamwork; there cannot be a moment's hesitation. I placed
the figures and objects carefully to form interesting rhythms,
creating, at the same time, a unified pictorial composition.*

138

The degree to which the form is revealed, of course, depends entirely on the thinness or thickness of the clothing material, as well as the looseness or tightness of the garment. A monk's heavy robe, for example, reveals very little of the human form beneath. Heavy material usually shows large simple folds; lighter material shows a greater number of folds. The texture of the material also influences the character of the folds: linen, for instance, shows a different wrinkle from silk.

While you are drawing and painting, you should search for the character and rhythm of the folds, giving variety to their shapes and directions. Render the folds broadly and simply, or they will take on greater importance than the figure itself. Eliminate the folds that confuse the form and action of the figure, as well as the folds that conceal the design of the picture itself. Drawing and painting drapery is difficult, but mastering it will contribute greatly to the success of your work.

COMPOSING THE FIGURE

Before you start to paint the figure, you must establish the drawing and design on your canvas. First pose the model in an interesting position, appropriate to her character. Since it will take some time to complete your picture, make sure that the model's position is not too strained and is easily resumed after a rest period. Choose a pose that the model can fall into naturally.

In the section on composition and spatial relationship in Chapter Four, I discussed the division of the picture plane: theories of space division which apply to all pictures, regardless of their subject matter. Whether you are painting still life, landscape, or the figure, your objects are carefully arranged within a given space. In a figure painting, another element is introduced: the movement of the figure or the *gesture*. The viewer is always keenly aware of the gesture. Improperly handled, the gesture can upset the picture balance entirely: an arm reaching out has significance and must be well controlled or it will force the eye out of the picture. Actions must find counter-actions.

Composing the picture, consider the shape and size of your canvas: vertical, horizontal, or square. Also consider the scale of your figure: if it is large, and appears in the foreground, the figure will dominate the picture space; if small, the figure will be only incidental to the main subject.

A figure in a standing position naturally requires a vertical canvas. A beach scene containing numerous figures can take a long, horizontal canvas, because of the horizontal shore line. A square canvas is often effective when you are painting a figure in an interior or a figure accompanied by an architectural motif.

Establish the center of interest in your composition: is it a group of figures, a single figure, or an object? The eye rests on this focal point. The surrounding areas are also important, composed in such a way that the eye enjoys the minor areas as well, but always returns to the center of interest.

When painting a group, be sure that the figures overlap and interlock, without standing out separately. In this way, the group assumes a unity that the eye perceives immediately. Within the same composition, you can use other figures, moving them away, or toward the central group. There can also be groups of less important figures on a different plane. This variation gives life and interest to your picture.

Every compositional idea has many possible variations. You should give careful consideration to these possibilities, making many pencil sketches, grouping, and regrouping the figures, paying close attention to the division of spaces, until you find the arrangement that expresses your idea best. You can even change the shape of the canvas to make the composition more important and exciting. There is no hard and fast rule. Your sense of balance and imagination will be your guide; your critical sense will help you make necessary corrections when you find your composition unbalanced.

There are many subjects that you can paint: sports events, the circus, figures in the park or on the street, picnics, beach scenes; in short, any outdoor or indoor activity. Begin modestly. Start with a simple subject and evolve to the more complex subjects (like mythological or Biblical studies) only after you understand composition and have gained control of the medium.

Color plays a large role in the composition of your painting. Any arrangement of color should be well integrated so that it does not destroy the balance of the picture. Color should contribute to, and emphasize, the *mood* of the picture as well. Work out color relationships in small sketches, a process that will give you a clear concept of the message you wish to convey.

DESIGNING THE BACKGROUND

The background objects you select should be arranged so that they contribute to the composition and the central theme. From various drapes, select the background color that complements the figure. Depending on the shape and size of your canvas, try to divide the background, part wall and part drapery. You may prefer a landscape background, which you should merely suggest without including too much detail. At first, keep your compositions very simple, concentrating on the figure as the main motif.

A figure posed in an interior always makes an interesting painting. Use part of the room as a background, perhaps including a flower still life arrangement. If you are painting a nude figure, you might include her bathrobe and slippers in the picture for diverting detail and interest. Even when you

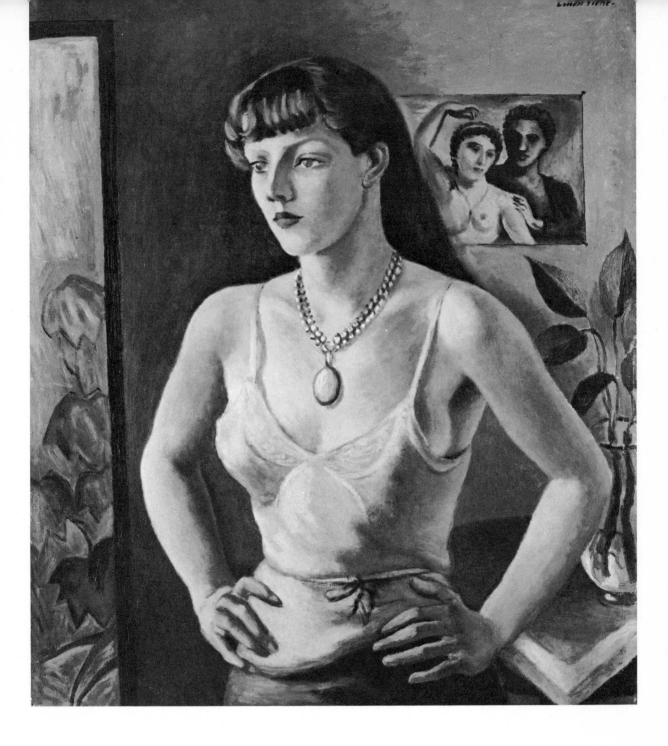

DANCER IN PINK CHEMISE *Contrasting dark against light is a device used to create depth within a painting. The surrounding objects complement the subject and enrich the composition.*

are painting a very simple figure study with a plain background, be sure to integrate the background with the figure in harmonious value and color.

In art schools and art classes, backgrounds are always a difficult problem. Screens and drapes help, but you must beware of a theatrical look. The art class also presents problems, because the background set-up is in the line of vision of only a few students. The other students must invent a background because they cannot see the real one. For this reason, classroom figure paintings are often uninteresting pictures. They have an art school look, which is difficult to avoid. I encourage my advanced students to experiment with backgrounds, to invent them or make studies at home. Interiors and furniture can always be incorporated in school studies.

STUDYING MASTER COMPOSITIONS

You can sharpen your perception of space and composition by studying the compositions of the great masters. You may not travel all over the world to see the originals, but you can find excellent reproductions in books at the library. Make it a project to pursue this study. Even black-and-white reproductions, small as they may be, are good for studying composition. Make tracings of the important shapes and movements, an excellent method of studying actions and counter-actions. Doing this will give you a greater understanding of space and composition. As you study these works, you will come to realize how varied and personal composition can be.

Nothing is accidental in the great compositions. Every detail is carefully chosen to contribute to the whole. Accidents may not be disturbing in sketches and smaller pictures, but in larger compositions, accidents are glaring. Studying composition requires thoughtful application, because it is the most difficult subject in art. Learn as much as possible about this subject. Your pictures will be more convincing for your knowledge.

DRAWING IN THE FIGURE

As you compose the figure, decide whether you want to include the whole figure or only part of it. Crop the figure in such a way that the body does not appear mutilated. I would not advise you to crop the figure at the joints: the arm pit, elbow, wrist, knee, or ankle. Cropping at the wrist or ankle is *particularly* bad, because the hands and feet always catch the eye, and the picture looks fragmentary without them.

Avoid doing an over elaborate drawing, finished to every detail. As a foundation for painting, a finished drawing might have an intimidating effect on you. In your reluctance to lose the drawing, you may fill in the paint like

THE DEBUT   *This is a life size figure composition of Elsbeth Rengies, a trapeze artist, with her father, Eugene. Although the "debutante" is slender and graceful, notice her strongly developed muscles. The rich red velvet cape and the rhinestoned costume contribute to a sparkling painting.*

143

THE CELLIST   *This is a painting in which I used interlocking and overlapping planes. The color is sonorous, consisting of rich browns, blues, and tans. (Collection, Dr. E. F. Ferholt)*

144

a coloring book. The result will look more like a copied drawing than a painting from a live model. In the process of painting, you may decide to alter the dimensions because the color gives a different effect than the black-and-white drawing. For this reason, focus the drawing on the general proportions and action of the figure; space the shapes well, and indicate the composition roughly. A casual drawing allows you to work freely with your paint and to build up the volume of the figure as you proceed.

On the other hand, do not make your drawing *too* casual. Often beginners make a very superficial drawing, even leaving out sections of the body altogether, because they are so eager to get on to the painting. Doing this is a great mistake, and generally leads to failure. The drawing and design on your canvas are like an architect's plan for a building: if the architect used a half-drawn plan and threw up a brick wall here and there, hoping everything would come out all right, the building would probably collapse. Take your time.

Check your drawing carefully for mistakes before spraying it with fixative. There may be any number of unwanted distortions: your figure may be too broad or too thick; the head may be too large or the feet too small; the figure may be broader on one side than on the other; one side may slant too much. It is easy to check the proportions of a back or front view, but side views are more difficult. Here you must watch carefully for perspective and foreshortening.

The balance of the figure is extremely important; it must stand correctly. The seated figure should be relaxed and fit well onto the object on which she is sitting.

After you have sprayed the drawing with fixative, run your finger over the charcoal lines; if no smudges come off, you know that the brush will not wipe off the drawing when you paint over the lines. You are now ready to lay in the paint.

LAYING IN THE PAINT

Lay in the large color areas, free from detail, to be sure your composition and distribution of shapes are correct. Many students start with the detail before knowing exactly where the figure is placed; then they have to wipe off all their work and start over again to balance the figure in the space.

On a white canvas, proceed by laying in all the shadow sections of the figure first, from top to bottom. Keep these colors darker than you think they actually appear. After you paint other colors in the background, as well as adjacent draperies and objects, these shadow sections will appear a lot lighter.

Next paint in the halftones and lights. Use large brushes, being sure to use separate brushes for the dark and light flesh colors. When the brushes get mixed up, as they often do, clean each one thoroughly in turpentine. This helps keep the flesh colors clean. On your palette, mix good amounts of the general *dark* and *light* flesh colors so that you do not have to mix color constantly. The halftone (a color you will need often) can be a mixture of the dark and light flesh colors. I say *general* dark and light flesh colors, because you cannot possibly mix a flesh color appropriate for *all* sections. Light falling on the body's curves and shapes produces many variations in tone and color, cool and warm, light and dark, in different sections. These variations require slight changes in the general light and dark flesh color mixtures.

Often beginners fear the loss of their drawing, leaving small white canvas margins around all the shapes. This results in an over-emphasis, separating each pattern and separating the figure from the background. Once done, this is often impossible to correct, because it is so difficult to match the colors and shades again when you want to fill in these blank areas. The student tries to blend these mismatched colors into the forms, repainting much of the figure. Then the painting begins to look spotty, generally ending in failure. I advise you to interlock and overlap colors from the very beginning. You can always find your outline again.

After the figure is simply laid in, begin painting the background. Lay in the colors next to the figure first, slowly approaching the outer perimeter of the canvas. This is important, because you are building form and depth. Do not paint flat background surfaces like a house painter; vary your brush stroke and texture, in order to give the feeling of air around the figure. Use different brushes for the background, keeping the brushes for cool colors separate from the brushes for warm colors. Wipe your brushes frequently on an absorbent paint rag.

You cannot judge your colors until your canvas is completely laid in. For this reason, do not attempt to finish one section before painting another part. When the paint is all laid in, correct the volume and color of the figure. Even the experienced painter will find many corrections to make at this stage, so do not be discouraged. Build up your figure broadly and only towards the end should you paint the detail.

In a full figure painting, delineate only the general character of the head. Bringing out the characteristic form of the face is more essential than concentrating on the eyes, nose, and mouth. In the drawing, the position of the features should be indicated. At the painting stage, construct the head, emphasizing the *volume*. In this process, the outline and detail of the eyes, nose, and mouth are blurred. The extent to which you delineate the features depends on whether you are painting a portrait or figure. Portraits, which I will discuss in the next chapter, require greater detail in the features. But such detail need not trouble you here.

Hands and feet always present a problem to the beginner. You must learn how to see them in mass. Many students, when drawing the hand, start with one finger, then add another, and so on. Instead of a hand, you have a bunch of carrots! Feet present the same problem. I advise you to block in the total form before dividing it into fingers and toes. Even in action, hands and feet must be seen the same way. It is far easier to do this than you would think.

The head, neck, torso, and limbs should be rendered in their basic shapes. Elaborations, surface detail, and muscular movements are incorporated only when you advance toward the finished painting.

MIXING FLESH COLOR

As you begin to paint the figure, your first question will probably be, "How do I mix flesh color?" The answer is not simple. One paint manufacturer has a color mix called "flesh color." If only there were people to match!

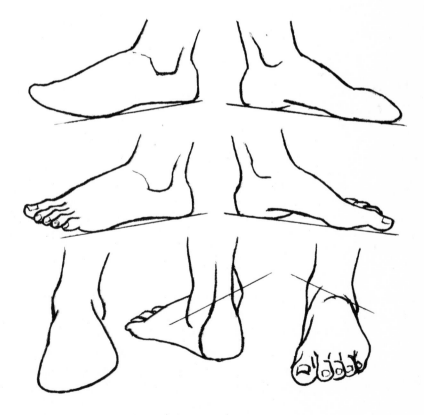

FEET   *If you regard the foot as a mass, you will have less trouble drawing it. Later you can divide the mass into toes.*

147

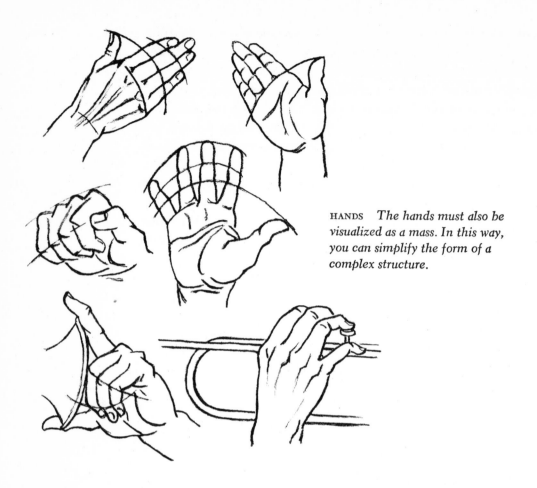

HANDS *The hands must also be visualized as a mass. In this way, you can simplify the form of a complex structure.*

There are *many* kinds of flesh colors. Even the flesh color of one figure may vary: the exposed parts of the body are ruddier than those parts covered and protected from light and air. However, you can work out the formula for a general flesh color, which will save you much time and energy.

For luminous flesh colors, I recommend a mixture containing cadmium yellow light, yellow ochre, cadmium red light, and white. The quantity of each color in the mixture depends on the particular flesh color of the model before you. Some people are pale, almost white in complexion. If the first mixture seems a little too warm for this pallor, cool it with viridian green or cerulean blue, being careful not to gray the color too much. Another good mixture for flesh color is raw sienna, cerulean blue, and alizarin crimson. For a ruddy skin color, substitute yellow ochre and venetian red or burnt sienna for cadmium red light. In light skins, there are many *silvery* tones in addition to the blue, green, and pink tones. Much of this variation depends on the light falling on the figure, as well as the color of the skin itself.

For shadows falling on the flesh, do not use the cadmium yellow pale;

mix yellow ochre, cadmium red light, and viridian green or cerulean blue and white. For the dark planes of ruddier skins, use alizarin crimson, yellow ochre, viridian green, and white. You can also use cobalt or ultramarine blue instead of viridian green.

To obtain the glow of skin color, keep your colors fresh, the same way you maintain the glow of any colored object in your paintings. Even if you mixed three shades of flesh color, from light to dark, and applied them indiscriminately, you would be painting in monochrome. Therefore, observe the nuances of tone from cool to warm: if the tone of the figure is warm in the light, it will be cool in the shadow. Remember that there will also be some *warm* planes in the shadow, just as there will be *cool* transitions in the planes of warm light. Studying modern masters will teach you a great deal about this subject.

The ears, cheeks, lips, nipples, elbows, and knees have warmer tints than the rest of the body. These areas should be sensitively indicated. Students often paint the nipples of the breast too dark, without blended edges, so that the nipples look like red buttons. Remember that even in the dark shadow sections of the body, the sensation of the skin color should emerge.

MIXING HAIR COLOR

The color of the hair is another important subject in figure painting. The approach to hair color is much like the approach to mixing flesh color. The possible variations of hair color are endless, even within the categories of blonde, brown, black, white, and gray.

Black hair painted only with black paint is very unsatisfactory: this causes the hair to drop out of the picture plane like a huge, dense spot. Observe the light falling on hair. To paint black hair properly, use ultramarine blue, mixed with burnt sienna. Use this mixture when you paint gray and white hair also. The mixture can be warmer or cooler, depending on the amount of each ingredient or whether you add yellow ochre. You can also obtain the color of dark hair by mixing viridian green with alizarin crimson. Brown hair is obtained by mixing viridian green with burnt sienna; the proportions of the two colors depend on the variation of brown you want to achieve. From pale to blonde to red hair, use the ochres, oranges, and reds, modified by various tints of blue, green, or black.

Hair can also be light-absorbent or light-reflecting, depending on its texture and gloss. For example, black hair generally reflects blue in the light plane. You must learn how to see the variations in hair color. The next chapter, which deals with portrait painting, will contain more information about this topic.

PAUL RENÉ   *Since this colorful portrait of my son presented such*
strong vertical movement, I divided the background horizontally.
Cropping the figure just below the knees is another sound
compositional device.

150

Proper handling of edges is essential: if the edges are too hard, the figure will not be enveloped in air, but will float on the surface of the canvas. Carefully rendering edges is particularly important when you paint figures against a dark background. The light edge of the figure should be blurred into the dark of the background. The experienced painter does this with a brush well loaded with paint; you may have to wipe your brush first. Experiment by using the *flesh color brush*, vibrating the light color out into the background space. The *background brush* would only outline the figure, cutting into and smudging the form.

A variety of edges—hard and soft—gives the illusion of light and air, and places the painted object deep in space, beyond the surface of the canvas. In some places, you can paint hard edges to accent the form. The soft edges you paint can vary in width, from a slight blur to as much as an eighth of an inch wide.

There are other ways of treating edges, and there are many concepts of form; this is a matter of personal emphasis. If you look closely at some of Renoir's figures, you will not see any edges at all; nevertheless, the form appears solid when viewed from the distance. In the still life section, I discussed the thick and thin blue lines Cézanne painted on the edges of his forms. Although he did not blur out edges, as I recommended you to do, he painted the lines so effectively that his objects stayed in space and air, without splitting the picture into separate units. Other artists, like Rouault, have gone to even greater extremes by painting heavy black lines around all their objects to achieve a powerful effect.

Thus, there are many ways of handling edges. However, when you learn to paint, do not go to extremes; keep your edges soft and learn how to distinguish between hard and soft edges in nature.

So far, I have discussed soft and hard edges in relation to the outline. Within the figure itself, there are soft and hard edges which you should delineate if you want to achieve unity. The lower line of the breast, for example, can be painted as a hard edge. As the breast line rises, it softens out until the edge disappears. The same thing happens to the edges along the spine, joints, and features.

Observe this particularly when you paint hair on the face. Where the hairline begins, the hair is thin: you can actually see the skin beneath the beginnings of the hair. I advise you to paint flesh color even beyond the hairline, then paint the hair delicately over the flesh color, only gradually increasing the density of the hair color as you paint the thicker hair, further back along the head. Otherwise the hair looks like a wig.

151

COMPOSING FIGURES IN A LANDSCAPE

The figure will always remain an important adjunct to landscape painting. In former times, the figure was generally the vehicle for telling a story: a hunt, a peasant wedding, a battle scene, or a mythological subject. The landscape was carefully selected to fit the story; nature and figures created and reinforced the same mood. Today, though far less common, story telling is still a valid subject practiced by artists.

How to use the figure in the landscape, and what scale, depends on the statement you wish to make and on your subject matter. For example, a street scene without figures would look empty and deserted, creating a feeling of loneliness and desolation.

The scale of the figure, in relation to the environment, is very important; this is a compositional device that can be forceful when well controlled, but incoherent and confused when left to accident. Again, the scale depends entirely upon your statement. A skier coming down a mountain slope might be miniscule in your painting, emphasizing the vast immensity of nature. Placed in the foreground, in another picture, the same figure tells a different story: the emphasis is on *man*, not nature. In an intimate barnyard scene, horses and cows would be relatively large. The same horses and cows would be quite small if you painted them grazing in a meadow.

In landscapes or city paintings, the smaller figures are incidental: they create a mood and enliven the scene; they must be placed naturally, adding to, not detracting from the picture. It is important that the incidental figures be in scale with the surrounding objects. The figures, in turn, give scale to the buildings, trees, and distant plains.

Observe the perspective. Separated by space, several figures in a landscape can be very distracting, so place them carefully. If you have a figure walking in the foreground, do not repeat the same movement in the middle distance. Place one figure in a doorway or leaning over a fence. Vary the grouping of figures overlapping the planes.

If your figure and landscape are not unified, you will have two separate pictures. Softening the edges of the figure helps to give the effect of a surrounding atmosphere. Work out a color scheme and composition that will envelop the figure and landscape in the same atmosphere.

The large figures in the painting should have their feet placed firmly on the ground, not too close to the edge of the picture frame. Leave a good margin between the top of the figure and the upper edge of the frame. This margin helps to keep the figure in space.

It is a very good idea to carry a sketchbook around with you and make drawings of all kinds of figures and animals in various activities. This sketch book can be your source material when you are in need of figures for your pictures. Photography is also a great help. Concentrate on the action, proportion, and volume, not the detail or likeness. In your picture space, the volume, color, and movement, well conceived, are more important than the accuracy of detail.

You can improvise the color of clothes according to the color scheme of your painting. In modern street scenes, vehicles, like cars and trucks, can hardly be neglected; but they are often difficult to incorporate because of their mechanical construction. Make drawings of them, in your sketchbook, relating them in size to the figures. Again, leave out as much detail as possible, or you will have a portrait of a car instead of a street scene.

ADDING FIGURES LATER

After your painting is dry, you can add individual figures. Sometimes it is difficult to visualize a new figure in its correct position. A good device is to sketch them in with soft pastel. If the additional figures are not right, you can easily remove the pastel with a damp rag. On the other hand, if you are *satisfied* with the additions, you can paint through the pastel lines, and take off the excess pastel margins later.

Another device for adding figures is to paint them roughly on transparent cellophane, then shift the cellophane around on the picture until you find the right place for these figures.

Chapter 10 PORTRAIT PAINTING

THERE is a widely held notion that the invention of photography has made portrait painting obsolete. True, in recent years portrait painting has gone into decline. But a photograph is only a substitute for a very bad painting.

For one thing, the value of a portrait is not in its likeness, although this is important, but in its aesthetic quality: form, color, space, texture, and composition. Moreover, a photograph is a likeness only in a superficial sense, like a plastic cast of a face. No photograph has ever achieved the character insight and the personality of a Rembrandt portrait, nor the life and animation of Hals.

The essence of portrait painting is that the person "come alive." You must breathe life into your painting, show depth in the understanding of your subject, and make an aesthetically satisfying picture.

CONSTRUCTING THE HEAD AND NECK

The basic mechanical problems in portrait painting are to render accurate physical proportions and to place the volumes of the head and figure in the defined canvas space. The proportions of the head, as well as the features of the face—the eyes, nose, mouth, ears, and chin—vary from person to person. Observing and delineating these individual variations results in a likeness. The depth of personality, the thoughts, and mood of the sitter, are reflected in the features; but this psychological quality cannot be painted convincingly unless the painter fully understands the physical dimensions of the head.

Let us begin with the basic construction, or blocking in of the head. An oval or egg-shape generally represents the front view. Sometimes, particularly in masculine heads, a cubical shape is used. Consider the oval the simplest, basic form, when you present the head in various positions. A straight line, drawn down the center of an upright oval shape, represents the center of the face in full view.

When this solid egg shape is turned, the straight center line moves in the direction of the turn and becomes increasingly curved, until it is absorbed by the outline of the oval. The greater the curvature in the line, the further the head is turned from a straight frontal view toward the profile.

Next, draw the hairline and divide the face into three equal parts. These thirds represent the distance from the hairline to the eyebrows; from the eyebrows to the base of the nose; and from the base of the nose to the base of the chin. When this egg shape is tipped forward or backward, these three straight division lines gradually take on greater curves, the same way the long center line does; the features become foreshortened and assume new positions.

Since the ears are placed on the center axis of the head, their location is not changed much by the head's tipping back and forth, but the relationship of the features to one another changes enormously. When the head tips forward, the features fall *below* the line of the ear; when the head tips back-

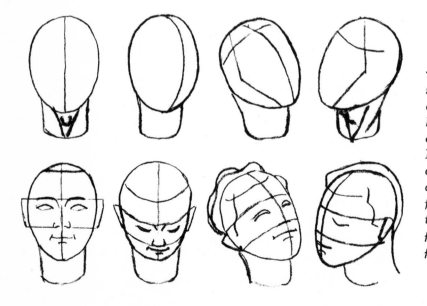

THE HEAD AS AN OVAL *You can simplify the shape of the head by drawing an oval, a method which helps you see the relationship of the features to one another. Notice how the position and curvature of the center line changes as the head is turned from full view to profile. Dividing the oval shape into three equal parts enables you to locate the position of the features.*

156

THE HEAD AS A CUBE *You can
also reduce the shape of the head
to a cube, marking off the position
of the features with straight
lines. Using the principles of
foreshortening, you can easily
locate the changing positions of
the features as the head turns.*

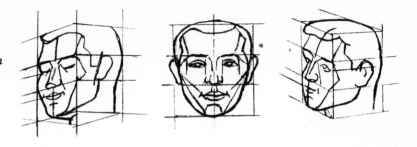

ward, the features fall *above* this line. The ear is the same length as the nose: the top of the ear aligns with the eyebrow line; the bottom aligns with the tip of the nose.

When you draw the head, you should carefully observe the planes: the face, forehead, cheeks, mouth, and chin comprise the front plane. The nose projects from this front plane. The side of the head is at a right angle to the front plane, bounded by the temple, cheekbone, and the corner of the mouth.

If you draw the head as a *cube*, rather than an oval, note that the front, sides, back, top, and bottom planes comprise the six planes that make up the head. Naturally, only three planes of the head are visible at any one time: most often the front and one side, plus the bottom or top (depending on the perspective, and whether the head is below or above eye level). Divide the features into three equal parts starting at the hairline, as you did with the oval head, but keep the lines straight. When the head is *partly turned*, the lines show the foreshortening: when the head is below eye level, the lines run upward; when the head is above eye level, the lines run downward to the eye level.

The neck is a column supporting the head. From the front view, the lines of the neck run straight down from the sides of the jaw. This cylindrical shape of the neck column is modified by the *mastoid muscles*, which run from the collar bones to the back of the skull, producing a triangular shape. The throat is located within this triangle. From the side view, you can see that the neck slants and is bounded by the jaw and shoulder lines. These muscles are particularly pronounced in athletes and in older people. The female neck, owing to the lack of muscular development, is more cylindrical than the male's and the muscles are less pronounced.

There are a great many variations in the shape of heads and necks: long, short, thin, and fat. There are also different head types and racial characteristics. Nevertheless, the *basic* muscular structure is always the same in all human beings.

PAUL WITH GUITAR   *This portrait is an excellent likeness. At the same time, the composition and background accessories add pictorial interest to the painting.*

158

The portrait painting student should acquaint himself with these structural elements and planes of the head and neck. Make many drawings of heads from life and from memory until you have formed a concept of the relationships between the head, features, and neck.

CONSTRUCTING THE FEATURES

You should know the basic structure and shape of individual features if you are going to paint portraits. There are innumerable variations. No person has features exactly like another's; personal variations constitute the personality.

When I speak of the eye, nose, mouth, or ear, I have a mental picture of these features, their normal or average shape. This so-called *normal shape* may not exist at all in reality because features vary so much, but the basic construction or anatomy is always the same. If you know the basic shape and construction of these features, you will have no trouble seeing and interpreting the individual variations.

EYES

Let us begin with eyes. In many ways, the eyes are the most important feature of the head, and the most difficult to draw. Constantly in motion, the eyes reveal the personality and mood of the person. Indeed, it is impossible for a person to conceal his mood; "looking someone in the eye" is the surest way to perceive his character and feelings. In short, the "life" of your portrait depends on your ability to draw the eyes.

The eyes should be drawn in relation to each other, not separately. The normal distance between the left eye and the right eye is the length of one eye. Protected by the frontal bone of the forehead, which is covered by the eyebrows, the eyeball fits into a socket. The cheekbone protects the eyeball from below.

The eye is set in a retreating plane, often largely in shadow; the upper lid is heavier than the lower, curving over the eyeball, overlapping the lower lid at the outer corner. The lower lid is thinner than the upper, on a straighter line, and is nearly stationary. When a person looks straight forward, the *lower* edge of the cornea meets the underlid, but the *upper* edge of the cornea is partly covered by the upper lid. The eye lashes of the upper lid are much heavier than the lashes of the lower lid; they shade the eye (casting a shadow), and protect the eye from dust and other matter. The upper lid is alert and closes quickly when touched.

Visualize the eyeball as round. In the front view, the iris is centered. When the eye shifts, or is seen on a slant or in profile, the iris also shifts.

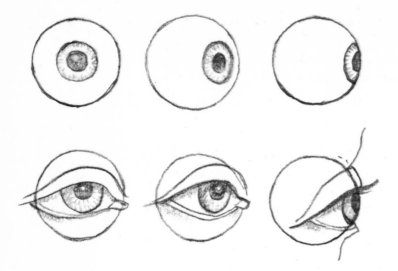

THE EYE AS A SPHERE *First visualize the eye as round, then draw in the eyelids. Notice that the iris is centered in the front view and that it shifts position as the eye changes direction.*

The eyelids follow the roundness of the eyeball, and perspective changes the eyelids also.

Concentrate on drawing the structure and general design of the eye from a model, not the many details. When you paint a portrait, keep the eye details to a minimum: observe the proper position, design, light, and shade enveloping this delicate structure. Keep the eye simple and suggestive.

Although the eye is very complex and takes on innumerable expressions and positions, you will be able to render the eye with greater assurance if you know the fundamental structure. So many beginners, puzzled by the eyes, draw a head in profile, with the eye in front view, just as the primitives and Egyptians did.

NOSE

The nose has a wedge shape; the form of the nose is a triangular pyramid rising out of the front plane of the face. Narrow at the upper part (where the nasal bone is located) and wider at the bottom, the nose continues as cartilage to the tip. The point at which the bone and cartilage join (the bridge) is prominent; the wider end of the nose, at the bottom, is triangular, forming the underplane which contains the nostrils. The curved wings of the nostrils connect this plane to the face.

The side planes of the nose move down from the bridge to the planes of the face. Note that these side planes of the nose are not straight, but bulge slightly at the sides of the bridge, terminating at the nostrils. The nostrils become rounder and thicker as they draw closer to the face.

160

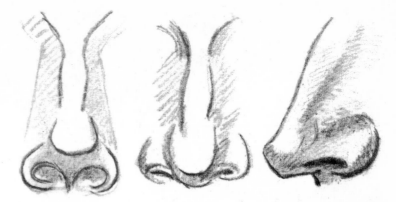

THE NOSE *The nose is narrowest in the upper section at the nasal bone, becoming prominent at the bridge. Note the slight bulge at the sides of the bridge as the side planes join the nostrils.*

Since the shapes of noses vary so much, it is difficult to describe the precise proportions and the distribution of each part. The profile accentuates these variations more clearly than the front view. Think of the nose as a three-dimensional shape, projecting solidly from the face and forming, at the same time, part of the total face structure.

MOUTH

The mouth presents a problem similar to the eye, because we cannot separate the mouth from the chin and underlying bone and tooth structure, any

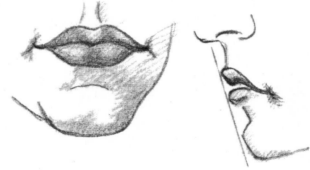

THE MOUTH *Notice the various planes of the mouth in full view, in the smile, and in profile. The upper lip protrudes slightly beyond the lower and is thinner and more delicate.*

MARIA LOUISE   *I painted this portrait of my daughter outdoors,
near a river. The face, in shadow, reveals nuances of
flesh tints contrasting with the sky and water.*

more than we can detach the eye from its surrounding structures. Like the eye, the mouth has great mobility of expression. The modeling of the surrounding muscles of the mouth is of primary importance, because the muscles establish the character of the entire lower part of the face.

The shape of the mouth and lips is largely determined by the shape of the teeth. A strong depression occurs between the lower lip and the chin projection. The lower lip is convex and softly rounded. The upper lip is comparatively flat and more angular, broadest in the center, and gradually diminishing in thickness as it retreats in a downward curve to the depressed corners. Observe the soft, depressed corners of the mouth.

The mouth, like the eyes, should be seen as a unit, not in its separate parts. Separating the upper and lower lip is the center line: a most significant line, because it reveals the expression of the entire mouth.

You can see the projection and thickness of the lips best in profile. Notice how the upper lip projects beyond the lower lip, how much heavier and fuller the lower lip is than the upper one.

In a smile, both corners of the mouth pull back; the lips part, revealing the teeth; the line of the upper lip becomes horizontal, loses much of its arch, stretches upward and backward over the teeth; the lower lip appears concave. The smile generally produces folds and dimples on each side of the mouth.

The mouth has many variations, like all features: full lips, narrow lips, hard lips, and sometimes barely discernible lips. The lips determine, to a large extent, the overall expression and mood of the face. When the corners turn down, the facial expression is sad; turned up, the lips create a happy expression. I once painted the portrait of a man whose lips turned way down, even when he was smiling. It was almost impossible to bring out a warm, friendly expression in his features.

EARS

Placing the ear properly is of great importance. It is probably the most neglected facial feature because, when seen from the front view, the ear does not project very far from the head.

The ear is usually located between the brow line and the base of the nose. The ear opening is just behind the middle of the skull. From the side view, the ear must be carefully related to the jaw and to the back of the head. It is often placed too far forward.

The ear is cartilage (with cavities and elevations which require your close study), divided into three parts: rim, bowl, and lobe. The hardest cartilage surrounds the bowl, attaching the ear to the head. The lobe, the

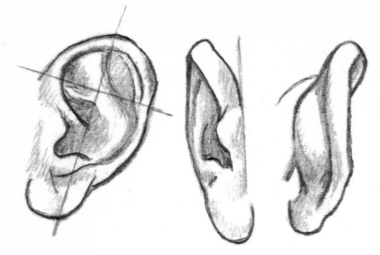

THE EAR *The ear's cartilage is divided into the rim, bowl, and lobe. The ear forms a complex design which should be studied carefully.*

softest part of the ear, is without cartilage. The rim and lobe are detached from the head.

The ear has a complex design of innumerable variations. Learn to understand it by drawing the ear from different views in its proper location on the head. Because of the many curves and details, keep the ear simple, rendered as a whole and by suggestion, or it will stand out from the head too prominently.

This discussion of individual features should help you when you construct faces. Draw people, all kinds of people; carry a sketchbook and make notes; observe people wherever you are and notice to what degree features vary. Ask your friends and family to pose for you and observe how their features vary from the norm. Create a head as a unit by drawing *all* the features *individually correct* and, at the same time, unified in the head as a whole.

Without a general knowledge of the head's structure, you will get lost in unimportant detail. Knowing their construction helps you delineate the features properly and bring them to life on paper or canvas.

PAINTING PORTRAITS FROM PHOTOGRAPHS

With a camera, you can make a dozen pictures and select the best (or most flattering) likeness in the time it takes the artist to set up his palette.

Some time ago, I was asked to do a portrait from a photograph because the subject lived some distance away and had no time for sittings. The photograph showed an average, middle-aged gentleman having no particular distinction. It just so happened that the man *did* come to town; I found him to have very distinguished features, and a lot of personality. The photograph did not resemble him at all! The photograph had probably been retouched, all the personality taken out of his face—even the features seemed changed.

I painted the subject from life, as I always prefer, and I often wonder whether his friends and family would have recognized him if I had painted the portrait from the photograph.

PAINTING PORTRAITS FROM MODELS

For the student, it is best to practice portrait painting from professional models, because they will not be too critical of the result. Professional models—available in most good art schools—can hold the pose for half an hour at a time and still be perfectly relaxed.

Many artists paint self portraits. In the absence of a model, this is a good practice for the beginner. You will soon get used to seeing yourself in the mirror—although a certain distortion takes place in the reflection—because you are seeing yourself in reverse. Often you will see self portraits of the artist painting with his left hand: this is due to the reversed reflection in the mirror. To prevent this inversion, some artists use two mirrors, doubly reversing the image so that the right hand is again seen as the right hand. This set-up is a little complex, but you should try it for experience.

After you have some practice in portrait painting, you can use friends and relatives as models if they are not too fidgety. Knowing them, you can attempt to interpret their personality in your painting. However, relatives and friends may be self-conscious, stiffening up rather than relaxing as they pose. They may also get discouraged and critical when they do not see a likeness emerging from your canvas immediately. They may say, "Do I look like that?" And they may tell you how they *want* to be painted. This mood transfers itself to you and may disrupt you, curtailing your freedom in painting. When the picture is finished, the sitter may consider it a personal offense if it is not beautiful or flattering. These are some of the complexities that you must anticipate in painting people.

POSING YOUR MODEL

As you pose your model, friend, or client for a portrait, there are several things you must consider. The most important aspect of the pose is the way in which it reveals the personality of the sitter. The pose must be typical: a characteristic way of sitting or standing; a gesture of the head or hands;

JOHN WAYNE AS "OLLE" IN THE LONG VOYAGE HOME *I painted this picture on the Hollywood set. By painting Wayne life size, I created a large picture, with just enough detail in the background to suggest the general mood of the scene. (Collection, Walter Wanger Productions)*

166

a movement of the eyes or mouth. Here you put your understanding and perception to the test. This may be easy with a friend; but often a client or a professional model is unknown to you and you have no time to study personality. Engage him (or her) in conversation; get him to relax; and look for a pose that seems to ring true, because the model's first poses will invariably look stiff and obvious. Take your time posing the model; there is nothing more discouraging than rushing into the painting, only to long for a different pose after the third or fourth sitting!

Since your portrait will require many sittings, the pose must be comfortable and easily resumed after a rest.

Faces are not entirely symmetrical; observe the slight variations of one side of the face from the other. The sitter generally knows which side is better and more characteristic. Select that angle of the face; it may make the difference between success and failure.

Do not place the model below your eye level, because doing this would distort the head, a difficult angle to manage if you are a beginner. In fact, the model's head should be slightly *above* your vision. This means that if you work standing, and the model is seated, you must place the chair on a platform about two feet high. An exaggerated view from above or below creates problems of foreshortening that the beginner would do well to avoid.

When you paint only the head (and in your first attempts, I suggest you paint only the head), seat the model in a tall chair with a straight back. This keeps the shoulders square and the head erect, much as they would appear in a standing position. Mark the exact spot of the pose with chalk: circle the legs of the model's chair and draw lines around his feet. Use the kind of chalk you can buy at the five-and-dime, or at the stationery store. This chalk will hold its markings for days, and yet will dust off easily from the floor or rug when you are finished with the sittings.

The head is such a complex form that a slight change of angle will quickly change lines and perspective. After you have established the position of the head, ask the model to look straight forward, his eyes focused on a point on the wall directly behind you. Focusing on a specific point is a device that makes it easier for the model to recover the same position. A certain amount of movement must be expected. In fact, I talk to my model while I am painting, because conversation relaxes the model and keeps the expression lively. When necessary, the sitter can always remain silent and resume the proper position.

Looking at a portrait, the first impression you get is very important. Although faces have a lot in common, there are great differences between them. It is easy to place faces in different categories: long and lean, broad and fat, strong or delicate, homely or beautiful. The overall quality of these variations must be well established. Your goal should be accentuation rather than flattery. You must search the character closely and show what kind of personality you are painting.

POSING THE HANDS

In a portrait that is three-quarter length or more, consider how you should place and treat the hands. Properly painted, they can reveal the character of the subject as they do in the great portraits by Rembrandt, Van Dyck, and Sargent.

Do not give too much gesture to the hands, but let them rest naturally on the chair, or on the body. Do not crop the fingers or paint them touching the frame. To avoid monotony, vary the action of each hand. Although hands are an important expression of the personality, do not let them detract from the face itself. Observe the paintings of Rembrandt and study the way in which the hands were kept unobtrusive by being painted several shades darker than the head.

COMPOSING THE PORTRAIT

Make your composition interesting. Pay attention to the silhouette and to the large shapes, using colorful clothes, still life accessories, or part of an interior, to make the picture more significant and to add interest beyond the person portrayed. Remember that environment says a great deal about the sitter's personality.

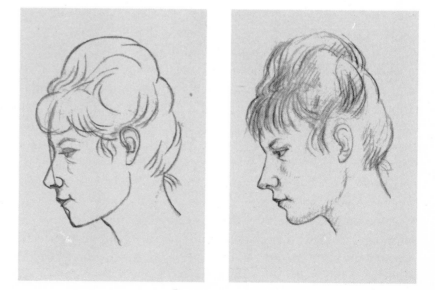

In the chapter on still life painting, I spoke of objects that go well together in creating a mood. You must also consider compatible objects in a portrait painting. The selection of clothes and accessories is very important. I ask my sitter to bring two or three costumes which suit him (or her) best; from these, I select one costume which, in terms of color and design, expresses the sitter's personality and makes the picture most interesting. These accessories often express the personality as well as the face does.

The problems of composing portrait paintings are similar to the problems in figure painting. When you paint a head on a very small canvas, the head fills most of the area, without requiring much background. A good canvas size for a head and shoulder portrait is anywhere from 16″ x 20″ to 22″ x 26″. Normally, portraits are painted on a vertical canvas, but sometimes a horizontal shape can be effective.

Avoid placing the head in dead center, and allow more space below the head than above. If you place the head to one side, be sure that you use some compositional device to balance the picture. The top of the head should not touch the frame, but should be a reasonable distance away from the edge to give the feeling of surrounding air.

If you are painting a profile, do not place the head in the center of the canvas. Allow more background space in front of the face, and less in back. Doing this prevents the observer's eyes from being directed out of the picture. Also apply this principle to the three-quarter length portrait. Establish a balance. Although you allow more space in front of the face, do not allow the back of the head to touch the frame. Do not cramp the figure; allow enough space to give the illusion of free motion on the canvas.

POSITIONING THE HEAD *When you compose your portrait painting, study the relationship of the head to the size and shape of the canvas. Line up the profile as an arc, showing the action of the curved line in relation to the rest of the canvas space. Also be sure the size of the head is appropriate to the size of the canvas.*

169

PORTRAIT OF A YOUNG MAN   *Sometimes a bust portrait placed*
in a horizontal canvas—rather than the usual vertical canvas—
can be very effective.

There are devices for filling empty spaces in the background. Drapery, well placed, adds an interesting spatial and color relationship to the picture, for example. Design the drapery with varied folds, but do not allow the folds to fall too deeply or prominently, detracting from the figure. For larger canvases, you can include a part of the room interior or a still life arrangement to fill background space.

The pattern of light and shade is an important element in portrait composition. Volume is created by painting the light side of the face and figure against a darker area, and painting the dark section of the head silhouetted against a lighter tone of the same background. This device forms a simultaneous contrast, bringing out the forms forcefully. The same compositional device can be applied to clothes; light clothes against a darker background or dark clothes against a light background. The artist must be careful when he uses these compositional devices, being sure to preserve a unified and decorative painting.

MAINTAINING DISTANCE

The distance separating the sitter from you has more significance than you probably realize. Six to eight feet is a good average distance, because it allows you to see the form clearly, without distortion. At a greater distance, the form, and perhaps even the *personality* of the sitter might blur. Closer than six feet, the sitter can exert too strong an influence on the artist. Portraitists have learned by experience that painting too close to the model can lead to a personality clash, which can be detrimental to the portrait. The painter should exercise his powers of observation without the mental influence of the sitter. In a commissioned portrait, the client often wants to be a back-seat driver.

Portrait painters place a mirror behind them, to help them compare the picture and the model. Seen in reverse, the faults are more easily recognized. I often put my mirror in a place where the sitter can observe my progress in the painting. This helps, because sitters can become bored when the artist is deeply involved in his work.

PROPER LIGHTING FOR THE PORTRAIT

Lighting is an important factor in the portrait, but it poses special problems: the light should fall from above or from the side of the model, *not* from below the head. In the beginning, avoid direct sunlight, because it will cause excessive glare and shadow, difficult for the beginner to manage. Since the lighting should accentuate the form of the head, the face should be predominantly in light and only partly in shadow. I would not advise the beginner to place the head in too much shadow, especially when using artificial light.

In daylight, sittings should always be at the same hours because the light changes direction and color at different times of the day. Shadows, especially when they are long and dark, tend to make a person look older. For that reason, always paint a young woman or child in full light with a minimum of shadow. Observe the cast shadows under the eyes and under the nose; make sure that the shadows do not distort forms. A long shadow falling under a nose makes the nose look larger than it actually is. Arrange the light and shade so that they delineate the planes of the face, rather than confuse them.

DRAWING IN THE PORTRAIT

After you have posed the model, and arranged the accessories and lighting, draw the picture on your canvas.

Shading and values in a head and figure are very subtle, but you must establish a correct relationship of the values in your painting at the drawing stage. Charcoal is an ideal medium for doing this. After establishing the general composition and basic forms of your painting, proceed to draw the shadows and determine your value relationships. Spray the charcoal lightly with a fixative (too much fixative will make the surface slick) and proceed to paint in monochrome, since color will only confuse you at this point.

In another section of this book, I discussed underpainting: a general monochrome painting of the composition. You may prefer underpainting to drawing in with charcoal. Try different methods of underpainting until you find one that suits you best—or if underpainting suits you at all. This is a very important phase of your portrait painting.

LAYING IN THE COLOR

When the underpainting has dried or when the charcoal drawing is fixed, you can proceed with color. As you shall see at a later stage, a face is not all one color. In the beginning, however, keep your painting simple: mix two batches of "flesh" color, one for light and one for shadow areas (darker and cooler). In the chapter on figure painting, you can find the ingredients I recommend for flesh color mixtures.

First lay in the shadow areas. The side planes represent one value and the under planes (under the chin, nose, and brows), represent a still darker

PORTRAIT OF PAUL   *This composition, with its still life accessories,*
could be called classical. The objects were carefully placed in
relation to one another and carefully delineated.

MIRROR REFLECTION   *I painted this self portrait with two mirrors*
showing front and back views. You will be surprised what
effects you can obtain by using one or two mirrors.

value. After you have done this, paint in the light tones, disregarding the highlights for the moment.

In your lay-in, therefore, you have established the volume of the head and suggested deep space. Let me remind you again to use different brushes for the lights and darks, and to keep the brushes clean to maintain fresh color. Too often, the student finds his painting gray and muddy, and his attempts to add color variations lead to disaster.

Now that you have blocked in the head, begin to block in the background. First paint next to the head, then work your way out to the edges of the canvas, always keeping the textures lively and interesting. Do not paint in the *whole* background until you have laid in the clothes and hands. Finish covering the canvas; keep the color fresh, the brush stroke broad; the color and forms simple; your light planes to a minimum. Do not worry about the subtle transitions of color and value. Working in light and dark patterns, simply indicate the folds of the clothing and the volume of the body underneath.

At this point, you must adjust your values. When you first laid in the head, you painted against a background which was different in color and value from the one you *now* have. You must make changes in view of the new color relationships. Even at this early stage, pull the picture together so that it achieves unity and harmony. After you have done this, your painting will probably be very wet and your model tired; so clean up and call it a day.

SECOND SITTING

In the second session, after the model has resumed the pose, begin to refine the modeling. Correct the drawing if necessary. In the first lay-in, some of the drawing is often lost, making it necessary to redefine the forms. Start with the light planes of the head and work towards the halftones, giving more attention to the transitions than you did during the previous session.

Notice that there is considerable variation in the shadow caused by reflections from the clothing and the background. Flesh, particularly in young women and children, tends to reflect the surrounding colors and lights, an effect which lends warmth and luminosity to the shadows. Be careful not to overdo this; the tonal variations are very slight, the color changes subtle. Overemphasizing the variations will destroy the unity of the shadow area and will destroy the form.

Observe color values in relation to the entire head, not just in relation to the adjoining value. A reflected light is never lighter than a direct light. Introduce variation into the shadows, but *keep them simple!* The details and

PORTRAIT OF MARKUS HANSEN   *I painted this portrait outside,
standing on a porch that overlooked a river. The day was
sunny, an atmosphere which cast strong shadows and revealed
the strong modeling of the face. (Collection, Mr. and Mrs.
John Hansen)*

176

textures of your painting belong in the light, not in the shadows. Refine your light areas, but do not put in your highlights yet. Hold back: save highlights for the very end, when you will probably discover that only a few are needed to do the job.

Do not complete any part of the painting at this session. Continue working on the entire picture at the same time; move around; do not become absorbed in details or in any one section for too long. You do not build a house by finishing one room and then starting with the next. At the beginning of a painting, a student often wails: "I cannot get the eyes right. Will you help me?" The plea is unnecessary, of course, because the primary concern at this stage should be laying in the basic forms and volumes.

In this second session, consider the smaller, more complex volumes: shadows under the eyes and under the lips; the cheekbones; the bridge of the nose; the ears; and so forth. Again, do not overdo any one feature or you will destroy the unity and form.

Next, paint the background and the hands to a more finished degree.

At this point, notice that the face is not all one color: there are transitions of warm to cool as the form turns toward shadow or moves into shadow; there are variations of color between people; and within a single head there are variations. The cheeks and ears are pinker than the chin. The side of the temple is bluer, because the flesh is close to the bone and the veins are visible. Just as the temple is different from the chin and jaw, so the neck is different from the face. Even a clean-shaven man seems grayer above the upper lip and on the sides of his face and chin. State these variations with restraint: giving them too much emphasis means the head will lose its color unity and its form.

You have accomplished a great deal in this second session, and now is a good time to stop. You may find that this middle stage requires more than one sitting, depending on the complexity of your painting and on your own working speed.

THIRD SITTING

When you resume work on your painting, you may find that some of the colors have dried in flat. Retouching varnish, sprayed or (if the painting is dry) lightly brushed on, restores the color and helps unite your new painting with the old.

A fresh look at your work may suggest a variety of changes in the drawing. Now is the time for you to examine the individual features more carefully. Painting the features poses special problems to the beginner. We will now examine these features more closely.

PAINTING HAIR

First, treat the hair as a volume in light and shade. Even the blackest hair will be light blue-gray under light. In the chapter on figure painting, I made suggestions for mixing hair color.

Do not attempt to draw in all the individual hairs; a suggestion of detail and texture in the light areas will suffice. Pay particular attention to the hair in silhouette. Even the most carefully groomed coiffure will show irregularities and stray hairs, which should be carefully observed. Pay particular attention to the point at which the hair meets the forehead; too hard a line makes the hair look like a bad wig. Note how the hair casts a shadow on the flesh.

The eyebrows pose a problem similar to the hair. Too often the student paints eyebrows that resemble Groucho Marx. The eyebrow has volume; it receives light and shade like any other object. Feel your own eyebrow; you will see that it does not exactly follow the line of the skull. Near the nose, the eyebrow dips slightly below the bony highpoint of the brow; then it goes up over the brow line and finally follows the line. Naturally, the eyebrow goes into shadow as it goes under the forehead. The juncture of all hair with the skin—including mustaches and beards—must be carefully and softly rendered to look convincing.

Avoid the temptation to make all hair one color and value. Careful observation reveals that the lightest value of the hair is often lighter than flesh itself.

PAINTING THE FEATURES

Of all the features, the eyes are the most difficult to paint, as well as to draw, but they are also the most important feature. Do not make them too linear or too detailed. Nor should you attempt to draw in the individual eyelashes. It is unlikely that from six to eight feet away you can see individual eyelashes. The white of the eye is white only in relation to the flesh color, but it is *not* a pure white; remember that the upper lid and eyelashes cast a shadow upon the white. The color is a low-keyed white, to which a touch of flesh color is added. The flesh color warms up the color; it will still appear white, but will hold its place in relation to the flesh color. The highlight on the pupil *can* be pure white; properly placed, the highlight makes the eyes come alive.

When you paint the nose, be sure not to paint the openings of the nostrils too black or too hard. Pure spots of cadmium red, as nostrils, add a warmth and luminosity to the flesh around them. Observe how Rembrandt, Velasquez, and Goya used spots of pure color, strategically placed, to enrich the flesh.

178

YESTERDAY, TODAY, AND TOMORROW   *This is a family portrait,*
showing my wife, Alicia, just two weeks before our son was
born. On the wall hangs a portrait of my mother who had died
several years before. This is a picture of intimacy and sentiment,
painted for personal remembrance.

PORTRAIT OF THE ARTIST'S MOTHER   *This is an intimate portrait
in which I painted the head on a large scale within a small
space. Whenever this is done, the artist must place the head
very carefully so that the small space can contain it.*

180

The beginner tends to paint the lips too red. A model wearing lipstick is no help; ask your female model to use a minimum of cosmetics. Note that the upper lip is likely to be in shadow, the lower lip in the light. Do not paint them as a smear of red. A moist lip shows strong highlights. If teeth are visible, render them simply. Overworked teeth can be very ugly.

If your model is aged, paint pronounced wrinkles with care. The wrinkles are probably not as dark as they first appear, so do not make them too hard or they will look artificial.

Do not paint the ears with too much detail. Unless they are simplified, their complex form can dominate the picture.

Do not paint *any* features in great detail. The human eye is not a camera —a cold objective piece of glass that sees everything in focus with equal detail, regardless of its importance. The human eye is subjective and sees in detail only what it wants to see. Therefore, finish in detail only what *you* think is important, only what is necessary for the statement *you* wish to make. You are an *artist*, not a copyist! Your judgment and perception allow you to capture the character and personality of the sitter.

I do not recommend that you paint subtle or extreme facial expressions because they are exceptionally difficult, even for a master. At first, concentrate on the physical, rather than the psychological, aspect of the features. If the features are well observed and delineated, the personality of the sitter will emerge; through the features and their relation to one another, the mind's reflection comes to the surface.

COMPLETING THE PORTRAIT

After you have painted the features, your painting should be near completion. A good artist knows when to stop. Do not tickle the painting to death.

If you have brought the entire painting along gradually, without getting sidetracked in details, you are ready to use your small sable brush to great advantage for painting meaningful accents: a glint in the eye, a highlight on the nose or forehead, a spot of alizarin red underneath the nose. If you had employed these accents earlier, you would have shot your bolt. Save them for last, ending on a bold fresh note. Make sure that edges which should be soft *are* soft, and that forms and volumes are properly realized.

Look at your painting in a frame. You are finished!

GROUP PORTRAITS

The double portrait and the group portrait present a far greater and more complex problem than the single portrait. Your relation to the single figure

JULIEN PLAYING THE CLARINET   *Here is an example of a cohesive
composition of overlapping planes. You should be careful
that these technical devices do not interfere with the central
theme of the painting. Also notice how the folds in the
clothes suggest the underlying anatomy. (Collection, Dr. and
Mrs. E. F. Ferholt)*

is direct: regardless of its gesture, the relationship is between the onlooker and the person in the picture.

In the double portrait a new dimension enters: there is an added relationship between the personages in the painting itself. It follows that the more figures in the picture, the more complex the problem of relationships becomes for the painter. The artist must consider the figures in a unity, not haphazardly placed, or unaware of one another. The setting should provide the logic of the occasion; the reason for these personages coming together. They cannot be like strangers, accidentally meeting in a public place. This is why such compositions often tell a story or become genre paintings. The subject can be a dinner, a banquet, or a wedding celebration.

The subject of portrait painting is very broad and has many possibilities. Devices and techniques have been formulated over many centuries. Portraits exist in great variety. The theoretical approach to painting should go hand-in-hand with the *practice* of painting: study the masters, old and modern, and learn from them. Remember that technical facility comes with practice in *seeing* as well as practice in *doing*.

THE MAKE-UP *This is another version of the white clown, posed by the same model who appears in the demonstration. Note the careful adjustment of the design and spatial relationships. (Collection, Mrs. Carol Brandt)*

Chapter 11 PORTRAIT AND FIGURE PAINTING DEMONSTRATION

THE FOLLOWING demonstration illustrates my approach to portrait painting. I painted a circus acrobat in the costume of a band leader, called a "tambour" in international circus parlance. This subject is excellent for demonstrating portrait and figure painting because of the clown's costume and the picture's compositional and textural qualities. The painting should help you see how to use accessories to create an interesting picture.

The subject, Eugene Rengies, was not a professional model. Since childhood he had been a circus acrobat, a tradition in his family for several generations before him, and a tradition carried on by his daughter, who is a trapeze artist.

POSING THE CLOWN

Since I wanted to paint a costume picture, I asked Mr. Rengies to bring along an extravagant costume for the sitting: the "tambour" costume filled the bill perfectly. I watched him apply the make-up for his classic circus face, and then I asked him to relax in a large chair.

The first pose Mr. Rengies assumed seemed too sprawling. I removed his coat and tried a different pose: this one proved too static and colorless. I felt a leader of a clown band should have more vivacity than his second pose suggested. I placed the coat in the background, changed the angle of the hat, and handed him his tambour stick. This change produced a lively

FIRST POSE   *The clown originally assumed this position as he settled into an easy chair. After studying the model, I decided that the pose was too sprawling and lanky to make an interesting composition.*

SECOND POSE   *This second pose, with the coat removed and the posture straightened, seemed too lifeless for a clown, and lacked vitality and color.*

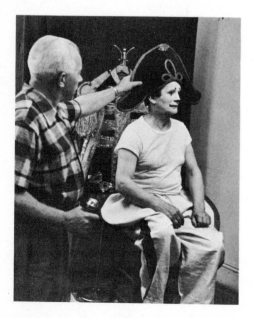

FURTHER ADJUSTMENTS   *Shifting the angle of the hat and hanging up the coat behind the model, I placed the clown in a more lively composition. Seated on a stool, the clown assumed an alert attitude, more befitting to a leader of a clown orchestra.*

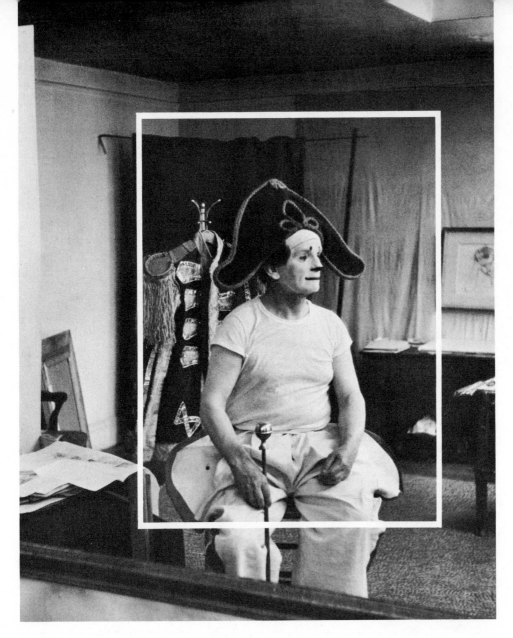

SIMPLIFYING COMPOSITION   *When I cropped the picture, I
eliminated much of the towering ceiling, the confusing horizontal
lines of the furniture, and the awkward folds of the lower pantaloons.*

upthrust action in the figure, an action that suited the subject and made an
interesting composition.

When I composed the picture, I excluded the ceiling (because it dwarfed
the figure), the furniture jutting in on either side (because it introduced
distracting horizontals), and the lower part of the pantaloons (because it
created clumsy and repetitious shapes).

187

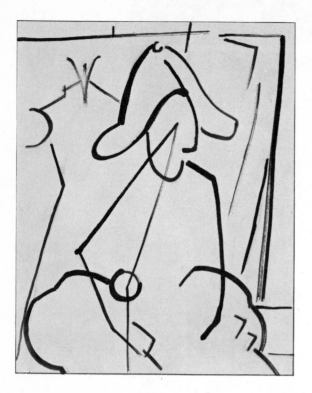

COMPOSITIONAL ANALYSIS *This quick sketch shows the movement of the composition: the thrusts and counter-thrusts of vertical, horizontal, and diagonal lines, modified by rhythmical round shapes.*

ROUGH SKETCH ON CANVAS *Using ordinary white chalk, I roughly sketched the portrait on my 34" x 44" canvas. Even in this early stage, I can visualize the painting. By wiping the surface with a clean rag, I can remove any chalk marks to make corrections. Later, when I paint over the drawing, the chalk will not discolor the paint.*

CASEIN UNDERPAINTING
I then painted over the chalk outlines with chrome oxide green casein. This underpainting is the foundation for succeeding layers of paint.

SKETCHING IN THE COMPOSITION

A quick diagrammatic sketch of the composition reveals the movement of the figure: the linear pattern and compositional thrust of the figure are directed forward and upward, toward the upper right hand corner, moving towards the viewer's eye. This forward movement is modified by an opposing diagonal: a broken line running from the upper shoulder of the hanging coat, to the shoulder at the right of the figure. The round shapes of the pantaloons add harmony and weight to the lower part of the composition, serving, at the same time, as a relief to the rigid linear structure.

With ordinary white chalk, I freely outlined the figure on a 34″ x 44″ canvas. Using chalk, I was able to visualize the figure quickly and make corrections easily, without spoiling the canvas. Later, when I painted over the drawing, the chalk left no discoloration.

UNDERPAINTING WITH CASEIN

Beginning with the head, I painted over the white chalk outlines with chrome oxide green casein. After using a sable brush to outline the figure and coat, I switched to a large, flat bristle brush. With the bristle brush, I applied a lighter shade of chrome oxide green, mixed with white, to all the shadowed areas. Some artists use grays or browns for underpainting. I prefer this chrome oxide green, because it is an airy color which beautifully complements the warm tones. The green, shining faintly through flesh color, gives the skin tone a pleasant, cool modulation.

Although the underpainting defines the shadowed parts of the figure and provides the foundation for all subsequent coats of paint, it does not show in the finished picture.

Since the casein tempera contains a milk base, its chemistry is different from oil paint; therefore, the casein underpainting does not combine with the subsequent layers of paint as an oil underpainting would. No matter how many times I scrape off or change the later layers of paint, the tempera foundation still remains intact.

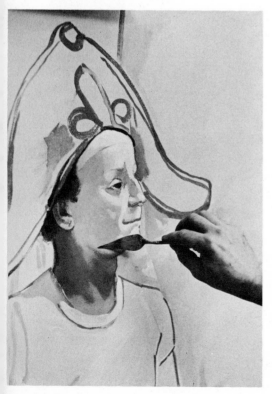

FIRST OIL PAINT APPLICATION   *I first applied the paint in the shadow areas with a brush, then scraped down the light-catching ridges with a palette knife. The paint is thin (lean) in the shadows. I made thick (impasto) applications of paint in the light planes with a bristle brush.*

190

USING A MIRROR   *I used a mirror to produce a more intense suggestion of depth and form. If I step back from my painting, I can compare the painting, mirror reflection, and model. Doing this gives me a feeling for the composition as a whole.*

CLOSE-UP OF MODELING *In this detail, you can see the three stages of modeling: the flesh outlined; the strongest shadows filled in with dark flesh tone and the light planes painted flat; the edges finally blended in, with the addition of highlights.*

LAYING IN THE COLORS

I applied my oil paint in the traditional method: thick (impasto) in the light planes; thin (lean) in the shadows. I painted an off-white thickly with a bristle brush on the light side of the face. On the shadowed side of the face, I brushed on a gray (of a thinner consistency than the white), then scraped it down with the palette knife to eliminate the light-catching ridges. I followed the same procedure with the flesh tones of the neck.

Throughout the painting, I often stepped back in order to get the effect of the composition as a whole. I used a mirror in the studio as a means of obtaining a stronger sense of depth and form.

After laying in the face, neck, and arms, I painted the hat and parts of the coat in alizarin red, and filled in various shades of whites on the shirt and pantaloons. Then I introduced the adjacent background colors: light blue at the right, and dark blue at the left. These colors, against the pure white of the canvas, appear quite different in character after new colors are introduced in the surrounding background. The more colors introduced, the more adjustments have to be made.

After I brushed the blues around the hat, the alizarin color appeared too heavy and I repainted the hat a lighter red. Following that change, I had to adjust the background by adding green to the background blue. In making these adjustments, I worked over the entire canvas without completing any one section.

MODELING

In three steps I modeled the drapery and hands: in the flesh areas, I first outlined the shapes with a round sable brush. Then I filled in the deepest shadows with the darkest flesh tone, and flatly painted in the lighter planes. In the last step, I blended the edges with halftone, and added the highlights. I used the same type of three-quarter inch flat bristle brush for everything except the outlining.

On the pantaloons, I suggested only those folds which emphasized the action of the figure. Later, I blended the high paint ridges with a brush to differentiate the textural character of the pantaloon fabric from the material of the shirt.

Originally, I modeled the structure of the face, before adding any of the clown's make-up markings on the eyes, nose, and mouth. When painting the underlying form, I did not want to be distracted by the surface pattern of his make-up. Although these patterns appear black on the painting, they were actually painted with a mixture of alizarin red and ultramarine blue. I deliberately emphasized the forehead band of the wig and the mask-like division between the flesh color and the white make-up on the face.

At this time, I made several changes. As I filled in the splashes of red and white on the clown's coat, I felt that the adjoining drapes seemed vague

PAINTING THE MAKE-UP   *At this stage, I painted in the make-up. Until this point, I was concerned with the structural modeling of the face as a whole and did not want the cosmetics to confuse the form.*

and without character. To correct this, I gave a definite pattern to the zig-zagging green drape on the left. I then filled in the background on the right, bringing the light blue drapes all the way down to the edge of the table. (Although the figure was actually sitting on a stool, I changed his seat to a table in the painting.) The strong horizontal line of the table top arrests the downward plunge of the arms and legs, a line which tended to lead the eye out of the picture. Making each shape more definite also affected the flesh tones: I accented the tones with highlights, and added reflected light along the dark edges of the flesh. Shadows are never dead areas; they are always full of color and reflections.

STRENGTHENING SHAPES AND MODELING *I then strengthened the shapes and the modeling, adjusting my colors as I proceeded. I accentuated the pattern of the blue and green drapes, and accentuated the flesh tones by adding highlights and reflected lights. Changing the stool to a table, I partially arrested the vertical movement of the arms and legs with a horizontal line.*

These two diagrams show the placement of the color patterns in my portrait painting.

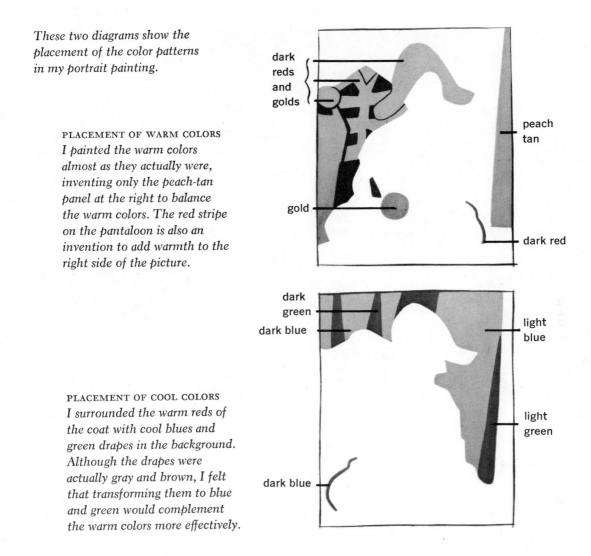

PLACEMENT OF WARM COLORS
I painted the warm colors almost as they actually were, inventing only the peach-tan panel at the right to balance the warm colors. The red stripe on the pantaloon is also an invention to add warmth to the right side of the picture.

PLACEMENT OF COOL COLORS
I surrounded the warm reds of the coat with cool blues and green drapes in the background. Although the drapes were actually gray and brown, I felt that transforming them to blue and green would complement the warm colors more effectively.

WARM AND COOL COLORS

Placing the warm colors, I painted the reds and golds of the costume almost as they actually appeared, making only slight adjustments in tone. I improvised a tannish-orange panel at the right to introduce some warm color on that side of the picture. I also invented the red stripe on the pantaloon to complement the large areas of red at the left of the picture.

I substituted the blues of the background for the actual gray and brown color of the drapes as they appeared in the real scene. This was not altogether an arbitrary adjustment, because when the eye sees a color, it tends to see the opposite color in the surrounding area. I saw the drapes as a cool color because of the warm reds of the coat hanging in front of the drapes. I always feel free to change colors to strengthen the overall expression of the picture.

THE FINISHED HEAD *Here is the completed portrait head. By painting the fur with short, thick brush strokes, I was able to contrast its texture with the smooth hat. The patterns surrounding the head have been clearly established, emphasizing a highly colorful, though not too heavy pattern.*

COMPLETING THE PORTRAIT

In the final stage, I strengthened the textures and clarified the patterns. I suggested the character of the fur on the coat by overlaying short strokes with the loaded brush. This roughness contrasts with the velvety smoothness of the clown's hat, I opened up the curtain folds at the top to reveal some of the wall, adding more pattern and variety, and relieving any tendency to heaviness, especially important in such a highly colored picture.

I finished the picture ten days after the model first posed. Although I had painted Mr. Rengies a number of times before as a gentle, wistful clown, in this picture I intended to paint a clown maestro as a vigorous, assertive character. I was not interested in merely reproducing a subject: my objective was to give the clown human significance.

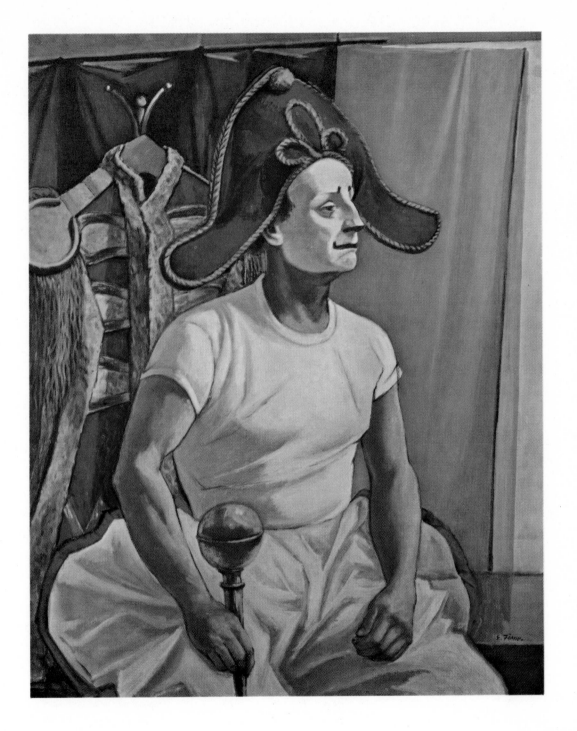

THE TAMBOUR *In the finished painting, vivid colors and strong thrusts and counter-thrusts help create a forceful, assertive personality.*

A FINAL WORD

I N THIS book we have covered the various aspects of oil painting and its technique, applied to still life, landscape, figure, and portrait painting: a very large range to survey in one book.

I have introduced you to the various materials and techniques traditionally used, and the theoretical concepts of space division, composition, and perspective. I could only touch upon some subjects briefly, such as anatomy and figure drawing. In the course of your study (depending on how far you go), you will study books specifically covering these subjects.

I have given you general concepts and considerations which you will adopt naturally in time. Do not let them intimidate you; work freely, doing the best you can. Studying your finished work, you will recognize where your mistakes are, and can either correct them in your painting, or avoid making them in the future. Do not labor on the same picture too long, especially if you are not using a model. Paint new pictures continually and learn as you progress with each painting.

Becoming an artist does not mean merely that you learn to use your tools; above all, it means learning how to see. As your powers of observation get better, your work improves.

So far, we have concerned ourselves mainly with craft and performance. To be an artist you must use your tools well, but you must also go far *beyond* the craft to achieve significant work. Your tastes and perceptions, formed early in life, are qualities that differentiate one artist from another. They

CONNECTICUT RIVER FARM WINTER   *In my studio, I painted this scene of a pre-revolutionary farm on the border of New Hampshire. The muted color tones bring out the winter silence at nightfall. (Courtesy American Artists Group)*

will have a strong bearing on your artistic expression. After you have mastered the fundamentals of painting, express yourself in your own way.

Works of art are never factual illustrations or camera-eye reproductions of any scene: your personality and imagination will *transform* reality, putting it on a higher plane. Realizing a subject is realizing one's self: it is *you*. Alone in your studio, with a subject to render, you can explore all your potentialities. This is a matter of self-expression. Often you will discover accidents that are not accidents at all, but subconscious emotions you had long forgotten. This is what art is made of. You are not taught these things; you must be able to recognize the hidden forces within you and then use them to their full extent.

Pictures in museums, galleries, and magazines are a good means of study; analyze their composition, their color and values, and their interpretation of the subject matter. Studying these pictures, you will form sympathies and antipathies: a way of learning about pictures and, more important, a way of learning about your own self. All this will aid you in your goal: self-expression.

The saying, "style is the man," is very apropos. Life changes and we change with life. Our emotions and tastes change, and so will our work. Thus, expression is a matter of self-discovery: the further you go, the further you see. There is no repetition in good art; your vision should remain fresh and new, whether you paint from nature, memory, or imagination.

Learning how to see should be your main objective. That is how you will discover the beauty of the world, even in the humblest objects. Interpreting this world is the artist's mission.

Creative expression in art is as varied as individual artists; therefore, there can be no positive rule, or any single approach to the subject. There are, however, fundamental concepts and rules of picture making which have been distilled from a long tradition of painting. These rules are important to know; they help provide you with an approach to painting; they help you evaluate other paintings; what is more important, they help you to analyze and criticize your *own* work. I have incorporated these traditional art concepts in this book. Study them well and keep referring to the book as you progress in your painting.

The main thing is that you paint and keep on painting. You can learn only by doing; the more you paint, the more ideas will come to you. Supplement this painting by visiting galleries and museums to acquaint yourself with the various styles of old and modern masters. You will find your favorites and learn from them. Meet the artists in your community, and exhibit your pictures whenever you can. Doing this will help you to evaluate your work in relation to the work of other painters.

Self-criticism helps you improve your work. Do not worry about manner and style, qualities which will evolve automatically if you are yourself. Above all, have fun, experiment, enjoy your work, and learn how to see.

Art has come of age and, once again, the artist is achieving a position of status. This was not always the case. Old masters like Titian, Holbein, and Rubens were well esteemed by their fellow men. But in modern, "practical," industrial society, the artist has been regarded with suspicion as a long-haired romantic. After a dinner party, less than forty years ago, a man might say to me: "What business are you in?" When I replied, "I am an artist," he would nervously say, "then you must talk to my wife," and disappear.

How times have changed! Today statesmen, bankers, industrialists, and truck drivers are painting, thanks to the ladies who kept the torch burning (although women were once largely confined to painting delicate watercolors). Today everyone has the desire to express himself and painting is one of the important media for self-expression. Painting has become an important leisure time occupation. Never were there so many enthusiastic and inquisitive amateurs in art.

I say *amateur* advisedly, because art remains a great and difficult profession, requiring many years of study, research, and application. Some amateur painters, through perseverance and talent, have achieved professional status, a level which should not be the primary motivation for the beginner, however. Even among those we might call professional art students, only a small percentage continue through life as artists and only a very few achieve recognition in this field; but all are enriched by the experience. Self-discovery and self-expression are important rewards in themselves.

Since the artist no longer copies nature and the paintings of old masters, many "isms" have sprung up in recent times, almost to the point of utter confusion. How far can we go and what is the end? No one knows the answer. One thing is certain: man's imagination and ingenuity are as great an asset in art as they are in life. We must remember, however, that progress *per se* is not always an upward movement; sometimes movement is downward, as has happened before. When excesses in expression occur and become meaningless, they will be discarded sooner or later and adjustments will take place.

The tradition of painting and the traditional concepts of art will continue to exert their influence, providing basic lessons that every artist must learn. The traditions are the vocabulary of art, evolved since ancient times. In this book, I have endeavored to acquaint the student with this vocabulary and to give him the tools for self-expression. How he will shape this vocabulary into sentences, conveying a message, cannot be foretold. This will depend on the individual's application, personal taste, and talent.

GLOSSARY

ACCENT An emphatic stroke, dark or light.

ALLA PRIMA An Italian term for painting directly on the canvas.

PRIMA PURA A method of painting in which paint is laid on directly, not to be changed or overpainted.

ANILINE A brilliant color derived from coal tar, used as a dye; not permanent in oil painting.

BLEND To soften edges, to merge colors into one another on the picture.

BRIGHT BRUSH A bristle brush having a short, square shape.

CAST SHADOW The shadow an object casts on the ground or casts on an adjacent surface.

CHAMOIS A piece of soft leather used for erasing charcoal.

CHIAROSCURO Deep space in painting created through light and dark shading.

ECORCHE A picture of a figure shown without its skin, to render visible the muscles, joints, and veins.

FAT A coat of paint rich in oil content. The opposite of fat paint is lean paint, much diluted with turpentine.

FERRULE The metal tubing that holds the hair of the paint brush.

FIXATIVE A thin alcohol and shellac fluid, sprayed on charcoal, pencil, or pastel drawings, to prevent the surface from smudging.

FLAT BRUSH A flat, long-haired bristle brush.

GENRE PAINTING A painting of figures which tells a story.

GLAZE   A transparent color tint which is washed over a solid paint surface.

HUE   A word denoting sensation of color: red, yellow, blue, etc. Hue has no relation to the lightness or darkness of a color.

IMPASTO   A thick body of paint, usually opaque, applied with the brush or palette knife.

INTENSITY   Refers to the strength or weakness of a color (not to its hue).

MATTE   A surface without sheen; unvarnished.

MEDIUM   The liquid vehicle (binder) with which pigments are mixed by the manufacturer to form paint (oil, water, casein, etc.). Also the name for the thinner used by the artist as he paints.

MONOCHROME   A painting in which all tones are created with one color and white.

MOTIF   The subject you have selected to draw or paint.

NOCTURNE   A night scene.

OPAQUE   Solid color through which the viewer cannot see the surface beneath; not transparent.

PICTORIAL COHERENCE   Organization of design, color, spatial relationships, and texture.

PIGMENT   Color in its powder form, before it is ground with oil or another binder to make paint.

PRIMER   The material used for preparing (priming) a canvas or panel surface for painting.

REFLECTED LIGHT   A light which is produced by the reflection of another object.

SATURATION   A pure color has full saturation. The term is also used in mixed colors to indicate *comparative* saturation.

SCUMBLING   A non-liquid semi-opaque paint, dragged over a dry paint surface.

SKETCH   A quick study; this can be an oil paint sketch or a drawing.

STRETCHER   A wooden frame on which canvas is stretched for painting.

STUDY   A detail that can be incorporated in a larger work; a mural study, a study of a tree, etc.

TACKY   A paint coat that is not quite dry.

TONE   The overall value or dominant color effect of a painting.

TOOTH   Refers to the rough or smooth surface of a canvas.

VALUE   The lightness or darkness of a color.

WASH   Color much thinned with turpentine or medium used for laying in a picture.

INDEX